The Social Justice Advocate's Handbook:
A GUIDE TO GENDER

The Social Justice Advocate's Handbook:
A Guide to Gender
Copyright © Samuel Killermann, 2013

Published by
Impetus Books
Austin, TX
www.impetus.pw

Special discounts are available on quantity purchases by schools, corporations, associations, and others. Book also available in full color print and E-book versions. For details, contact the publisher at the address above.

ISBN 978-0-9897602-0-1
Cover design, layout design, and all illustrations
by Sam Killermann

First Edition, published August 2013
2 4 6 8 10 9 7 5 3 1

To Albina and Helmuth, without whom this book would not exist.

To Megan, who gave me the words I needed to see it to completion:
The, Be, To, Of, And, A, In, and [see, using that one already] That.

TABLE OF CONTENTS

OUTSIDE OF A DOG, A BOOK IS MAN'S BEST FRIEND. INSIDE OF A DOG IT'S TOO DARK TO READ.

—Groucho Marx

BASIC TRAINING

Learning the things every social justice advocate needs to know, before we get into the gender-specific material.

BREAKING THROUGH THE BINARY

Moving from a traditional, incomplete understanding of gender to an inclusive, cognitively complex understanding of gender diversity.

FEMINISM AND GENDER EQUITY

Taking a quick look at the most contemporarily prominent gender movement and how it aligns with a more comprehensive cause.

SOCIAL JUSTICE COMPETENCE: WORKING FOR GENDER EQUITY

From comprehension to competence, knowledge to action, thinking to doing—this section focuses on preparing you for social justice interventions and education.

APPENDIX

The more you know the more you know. Additional bits and pieces that help complete this gender puzzle.

BASIC TRAINING

CHAPTER I

GENDERAL ADDRESS

AS A STAND-UP [COMEDIAN], I TRY TO CHANGE THE WORLD. AS AN
ENTERTAINER, I TRY TO ENTERTAIN. AND AS A LESBIAN, I TRY TO
PICK UP THE PRETTIEST GIRL IN THE ROOM.

—*Lea DeLaria*

Attennnnnshun!

I have been ordered to lead this battalion into battle, and I have to say that I've never had the privilege of commanding such a finely assembled, almost-overbearingly eager, terrifyingly adorable group of soldiers. And I *know* privilege!

It's an honor to have you in this regimen, but we have a long way to go before you're battle ready.

Let's talk about the enemy: the no-good, good-for-nothing, but usually not actually that bad, layperson—and I'm talking the *layest* of the lay. We're up against people who wouldn't know privilege if it hit them squarely in the mouth on a daily basis or, like when privilege hits them squarely in the mouth on a daily basis; people who don't know their cissexism from their internalized oppression, and definitely don't understand — bear with me here, troops—that *one perpetuates the other*. I mean come on!

Now let's get serious.

There are rumors going around that some of the enemy have infiltrated this battalion. These laypeople are hiding among us, trying to learn our ways, to understand our battle plans and gender formations ... and you know what I say to that? *Bring 'em on.* Like Granddaddy always said, "Keep your friends close, but keep your enemies preoccupied by reading your secret military handbooks because maybe you'll convert one to an ally and have another friend on the battlefield, which is always nice."

Oh, Granddaddy, how I miss your eloquent way with words.

Enough talk. It's time to get into basic training. There's a war waiting for us, and wars ain't been known to wait too kindly.

At eeease!

Sam Killermann
Five Smile Genderal
Social Justice Forces

CHAPTER 2

NAVIGATING THE BOOK

I MAY NOT HAVE GONE WHERE I INTENDED TO GO, BUT I THINK I HAVE ENDED UP WHERE I NEEDED TO BE.

—*Douglas Adams*

First things first: I promise I'm done with the military references, but you should admit it was fun for that first chapter. *Admit it, soldier!*

OK. Now I'm done.

There is a lot to this book, and it may seem overwhelming if you try to take it all in at once, so I wanted to take a moment here to explain some things. I hope that's OK.

IT'S A HANDBOOK, NOT A NOVEL

Think of this book as more Noah Webster than Stephenie Meyer. While it's certainly more fun to read than the dictionary (and has way more cartoons and Star Wars references), it's not meant to be a binge-read over a long weekend while reminiscing on high school loves lost.

By all means, read it cover to cover if you'd like, but also highlight, fold corners, write notes, and treat it as a textbook. At the end of several chapters there is a blank page for you to fill with notes and reflections, so don't hesitate to fill them up. That's why they are there. You may need to read a chapter a few times before its concepts click. That's OK. Some chapters may not mesh well with your approach to social justice while others do. That's also OK.

This book is meant to be something you refer back to when you're unsure of whether you remember something correctly or when you're in situations where you're leading conversations about these issues and need some backup.

IT'S A GUIDEBOOK, NOT A TEXTBOOK

You know how in the last section I just said you should treat this as a textbook? You certainly should, but mostly in the physical ways you treat textbooks. You should not (please do not) treat this with the same academic prestige you would a textbook.

There are great textbooks out there about sociology, psychology, and social psychology (the pervasive themes of this book), and every year, more and more accurate scholarly books about gender are published. Those books are great at being scholarly textbooks about those subjects. This isn't that—neither is it meant to be that.

This is a guide to gender from a social justice perspective based on my understanding and synthesis of many of those books I mentioned in the last paragraph, a ton of other literary and scholarly writing by other folks, and also my firsthand research (i.e., conversations with thousands of people of as many different gender formations) and work in the field.

DO THE DRILLS

At different points in the book, I have included exercises. These may seem silly or make you uncomfortable (not an accident), or you might think, "Who really has five extra minutes?" But do them. That's an order, private! (Sorry...again.

I included those exercises at key points intentionally. They are designed to help you reflect on what you already know about this stuff and what you've been learning throughout the book and apply it all to whatever is being discussed at that point in the chapter.

Kierkegaard said, "Life can only be understood backwards; but it must be lived forwards." That's the spirit of what I'm getting at here.

Yoda said, "Do or do not. There is no try." That's a pretty awesome quote in general.

DRILL: This is what drills look like. Now you have no excuse not to do them. Gotcha!

In order to understand where I'm trying to take you, you need to first understand where you've been. We are all coming into this subject with different levels and flavors of experience, and it's important to address and embrace those.

So, to sum it up: do the drills, Padawan.

THE APPENDIX IS A VITAL ORGAN

Unlike in the silly human body, the appendix in this book is quite necessary for survival. I tried not to overload it with excessive info, so the things that are there are intentionally included bits and pieces that will help you tackle this book and further your understanding of these issues.

If nothing else, check out the glossary of terms. There will occasionally be terms that I will define in-text, but for the most part I will leave the definitions for the glossary. If you see a word and you think, "What the what?" there is a good chance it's defined in the glossary.

The glossary itself is almost its own little Social Justice Advocate's Handbook, in that you will rarely find such an exhaustive list of LGBTQ+ related terms defined all in one place. If "gender isn't just male or female" is a new(ish) or fuzzy idea to you, Appendix A might be a good place to start this learning adventure. Think of it like eating dessert before dinner.

TAKE THE CONVERSATION FURTHER THAN BETWEEN YOU AND ME

If you read this book, learn a lot, come to understand gender better than you ever did before, and never tell anyone about it, and I find out about this, I'll experience the equivalent of passing a kidney stone, but with my brain.

Please don't do that to me.

Talk to your friends about this. Bug your loved ones. Sit down to tea with your frenemies. Start a debate with a former or current teacher. Whatever your method, it's fine with me. Just make sure the conversation continues beyond us.

I'm doing everything I can to help pull my weight on this (beyond just writing the book, I mean). A lot of what you read here will be published in some form on my website, www.itspronounced-metrosexual.com. All of the graphics, comics, and other silly doodles will be available on the site, ready and primed for social network sharing, and you can even discuss a lot of the content electronically on the site. Plenty of e-options for you there.

Most of what I've learned has been through conversations with others. I encourage you to get out there and continue building on this repository of knowledge.

HAVE FUN, AND ENJOY

I do my best to make what is generally an at-best intense, at-worst depressing subject into something light, enjoyable, accessible, and fun. I take this approach because I, like Mary Poppins, think that sugar helps the medicine go down.

This occasionally puts me in hot water with some social justice folks, who think I'm not respecting the seriousness of these issues, but I can assure you that this is far from the case. I deeply respect the seriousness of these subjects. It's just that I also have a healthy respect for happiness, prefer focusing on the light in darkness, and think there is always room for a little silliness in life.

I give you my full two-thumbs-up approval to do the same.

HOWDY This is your first blank page. There are many like it, but this one is first. Blank pages are your best friend. Fill them with notes.

CHAPTER 3

DEFINING SOCIAL JUSTICE

IF YOU TREMBLE WITH INDIGNATION AT EVERY INJUSTICE THEN YOU
ARE A COMRADE OF MINE.

—Ernesto "Che" Guevara

My first year of graduate school, I took a class called Social Justice Education and Training. On the first day of class, our professor, the amazing Dr. Ellen Broido (check out her fantastic work on allyship, among other things), asked us a simple question:

"Do you think it's possible for us to achieve social justice?"

I'm already getting ahead of myself.

WHAT IS SOCIAL JUSTICE?

For a simple definition, consider social justice to be the following:

> *Social justice*: a status in society where all people, regardless of their individual identities and social group memberships, have an equitable shot at achieving success.

Working for social justice, or being a social justice advocate, means trying to educate people, informing policy, and creating a shift in group culture that will make institutions more accessible to people of all backgrounds, or at least of the particular background for which you're advocating.

Because social injustice exists across such a wide gamut, many folks find it easier to focus on a particular identity or identity group and try to advance that group's status, rather than working toward what might seem like an insurmountable goal of equity for all identity groups. These folks may still call themselves social justice advocates because the movement for social justice is an all-hands-on-deck, intersectional movement where innumerable small efforts combine to form one massive, synergistic movement that will lead to a more equitable society for all.

An even simpler definition of social justice: equity.

EQUITY VS. EQUALITY

You may have noticed my use of the word equity in place of a word you may have chosen (or seen used before): equality. This was no accident, I assure you. This is an example of what I like to call "jerk-proofing" my writing.

While the two words are similar, they are not synonymous. Equity literally means "the quality of being fair" or "impartiality." Equality, on the other hand, means "the state of being equal."

Accordingly, "social group equity" could be defined as a quality where members of all social groups experience equity in society; that is, they experience impartial access to societal resources. "Social group equality" could be defined as a quality where members of all social groups have equal status in society; that is, members of all social groups will have the same experiences and quality of life.

See the difference? It's subtle but important.

Social equity is all about access to success (wealth, education, happiness, etc.), whereas social equality focuses more on possession of success (everyone gets an equal level of wealth, education, happiness, etc.).

That's all to say that fighting for social justice is not the same as fighting for socialism, but the two are often conflated by opponents who (sometimes intentionally, sometimes ignorantly) mash the two into the same thing and take up a platform against "entitlement" (e.g., "Work hard," "No handouts," Yada, yada, yada).

Let's make this definition extremely clear: social justice means that all individuals, regardless of their identities or social group memberships, have *equitable access* to social resources; it does not mean that all individuals should *possess equal* social resources.

DO YOU THINK IT'S POSSIBLE FOR US TO ACHIEVE SOCIAL JUSTICE?

Now that we have that out of the way, let's get back to Ellen's question. Do you think it's possible for us to achieve social justice? (Answer yes or no in your head, and then read on to the next paragraph for the correct answer.)

The correct answer is an emphatic "yes."

Actually, I'm pulling your chain. There is no "correct" answer. It's an opinion-based question, after all. Most of the questions posed in this book will not have any one "correct" answer. It's all different shades of gray—but not in a gross way.

But I answered "yes" so many years ago, and I hope you did, too. Because, to paraphrase my professor, "If your answer is 'no,' what are you doing in this class?"

As social justice advocates, we have to believe that it's possible to achieve social justice. Otherwise, what's the point in fighting? If Sylvester Stallone's character in *Rocky* didn't think he would be able to defeat that beast of a man Apollo Creed, do you think he would have trained so hard, working tirelessly until he defeated him, and been crowned champion? *(Editor's note: apparently Sam has never seen* Rocky *and doesn't realize that in the ending Creed actually defeated him. We apologize.)*

Tricked you! I am the editor, sillies. The point is that you can certainly still work for social justice even if you don't believe it's absolutely achievable in our society, because every step in that direction, even the small ones, can build up and lead to huge leaps in the demarginalization of and increased access for oppressed group members.

So fight on, Rocky! It's OK that you didn't win. In fact, it's damned impressive you even made it that far considering you have a tiger's eyes. That must have been tough as a kid, not having human being eyeballs. I bet they picked on you so hard for that. Wait, I'm referencing the right movie, yeah?

I should probably go watch it.

CHAPTER 4

THE CYCLE OF OPPRESSION

THE OPPRESSED ARE ALLOWED ONCE EVERY FEW YEARS TO DECIDE
WHICH PARTICULAR REPRESENTATIVES OF THE OPPRESSING CLASS
ARE TO REPRESENT AND REPRESS THEM.

—*Karl Marx*

Oppression is the exercise of authority or power in an unjust manner. Oppression plays out between social groups when one group has power and limits another group's access to that power.

DRILL: Take five minutes, with a group or by yourself, and write down all the things that come to your mind when you hear the word "oppression." Don't define it necessarily, just record all the word associations and concepts that run through your mind as you think about the term.

Oppression is the key roadblock in the way of achieving social justice. There are a number of ways to understand oppression, but we're going to focus on a cyclical model of oppression conceived by Sheri Schmidt.

Schmidt visualized oppression as a perpetual cycle where members of society knowingly and unknowingly participate in advancing oppressive attitudes and behaviors in a manner that progressively builds upon itself, like a really depressing snowball rolling down a really depressing hill.

This is an incredibly useful manner of looking at oppression because it helps you understand how the different elements of oppression interact and gives you a better sense of why it's so prevalent from generation to generation.

To understand the Cycle of Oppression, let's first discuss the various components.

STEREOTYPE

A stereotype is a preconceived or oversimplified generalization about a group of people or particular identity. Stereotypes can be negative or positive (in a later chapter I'll address so-called "positive" stereotypes, but for now, let's move on) and are taught to us by peers, parents, and other social groups and reinforced through social interactions.

A common example of a "negative" gender stereotype is "girls are bad at sports"; on the flip side of that, a "positive" stereotype is "boys are good at sports." Hooray! I'm good at sports! Someone, please tell my fifth grade basketball coach because I can assure you he didn't realize this.

> DRILL: Take five minutes and write down as many stereotypes about a particular group (ideally a gender-based group) as you can think of. Go as fast as you can, don't judge yourself, and see how many you can come up with.

In the Cycle of Oppression, stereotypes serve as the basis for our formation of...

PREJUDICE

Like a stereotype, a prejudice is a preconceived or oversimplified generalization about a group of people or a particular identity. What separates the two is that a prejudice is a conscious or subconscious negative or otherwise limiting belief about a group.

A common example of prejudice is the belief women aren't capable of being successful bosses and are better suited for or prefer detail-oriented work. This prejudice totally makes sense though (does it?) because, *stereotypically speaking*, a successful boss is someone who is trustworthy, a good listener, able to empathize with their employees, and a strong multitasker (hold on a sec...), which are all *obviously* "man" qualities (oh, wait).

Continuing the cycle, when an individual knowingly or unknowingly acts on their prejudicial belief, we get...

DISCRIMINATION

Discrimination occurs when an individual has prejudice and power and uses that power to unfairly deny access to or limit someone's ability to obtain resources because of that person's identity. Discrimination happens on an individual level; that is, from one individual to another (rather than from a group to an individual).

An example of discrimination is a person giving a job to an unqualified cisgender person in place of a qualified trans* person (which is generally legal, by the way).

And when a social group discriminates against another social group, we get...

OPPRESSION

As I alluded to at the beginning of this chapter, oppression is essentially discrimination on an institutional or societal level. I cannot oppress you, but a social group with a lot of power (let's say...straight + white + cisgender + nondisabled + male) can. And even though I just so happen to be a member of that group, I am by no means in control of it.

An example of oppression would be a law that allows organizations to legally deny transgender people employment solely because of their gender identity (this is in fact the case in most US states and it's this lack of protection under the law that enables our example of discrimination in the previous section to be possible).

When an individual grows up in a society with oppression and adopts the oppressive perspective, we get...

INTERNALIZED OPPRESSION

This happens when members of a target group are socialized into supporting and believing the oppressive beliefs (stereotypes and prejudice) about one or more social groups they belong to (i.e., identities they possess).

Based on how naturally each aspect of this cycle flows into the next, you can likely see how easily someone could internalize oppression—and how dangerous this can be. The same way we are taught to hold oppressive beliefs about members of other social groups, we're being taught to think that way about ourselves.

An example of internalized oppression would be a girl believing that girls are inherently bad at sports and deciding not to try to be good at sports because of this belief. Internalized oppression sometimes goes by another name: "The saddest byproduct of a social influence in the history of the universe and now I want to cry."

When individuals internalize oppressive beliefs about themselves and then act in ways that support and reinforce those oppressive beliefs, we get...

STEREOTYPES (SECOND GENERATION)

A girl who doesn't try at sports (because she "knows" she can't do well) ends up being bad at sports, so all the boys point and laugh and think, "Gee! Girls *really are* bad at sports."

Transgender people who don't believe they are worthy of employment (because they "know" something about them is unsuitable for the workplace) and therefore don't look for legitimate work end up homeless or unemployed, and cisgender people point and laugh and think, "Gee! Trans people *really aren't* employable."

A woman who never asks for a promotion (because she "knows" the men around her are better suited for management positions, finding "evidence" of this in the fact that only 4.2 percent of Fortune 500 CEOs are women), and the men around her point and laugh and...OK. I'm done with these examples. I'm sad again. But you get the picture.

THE CYCLE OF OPPRESSION

So that's how it works. Those are the components and their relationships to one another. Now, how about a visual representation, in adorably depressing style?

We have an agreement?
Yes. Let it be written.
We will share this one common value.
One universal ideal.
So what about the rest?
Can we come to any understanding?
Uhhh...
Ummm...
Yeah...
No.
Just kill each other?
Sounds good!

CHAPTER 5

THE CORRUPTION OF THE GOLDEN RULE

IT IS TEMPTING, IF THE ONLY TOOL YOU HAVE IS A HAMMER, TO TREAT EVERYTHING AS IF IT WERE A NAIL.

—*Abraham Maslow*

Have you ever heard the term "trigger" used in a social justice context? Basically, a trigger is a situation, word, or action that "triggers" an intense (and often destructive) emotional response in someone.

The Golden Rule is a huge trigger for me, so writing this chapter is going to be intense. I'll try my best to keep calm.

THE GOLDEN RULE

The Golden Rule is considered one of the most basic, universal social laws governing human interaction. It has religious origins and dates back thousands of years to Babylon (which was more than just a pretty garden), but unlike most religious tenets, it is practiced and celebrated by atheists and theists alike. Awesome.

In case you're somehow unfamiliar, the common understanding and application of the Golden Rule is "Do unto others as you would have them do unto you."

To really drive home the universality of this, let's look at how different versions of the Golden Rule are presented in the world's religions. Don't worry. I've only seen a couple examples of it cropping up.

Baha'i Faith: "Lay not on any soul a load that you would not wish be laid upon you, and desire not for anyone the things you would not desire for yourself." (Baha'u'llah, Gleanings)

Buddhism: "Treat not others in ways you yourself would find hurtful." (Udana-Varga 5.18)

Christianity: "In everything, do to others as you would have them do to you; for this is the law and the prophets." (Jesus, Matthew 7:12)

Confucianism: "Do not do to others what you do not want done to yourself." (Confucious, Analects 15.23)

Hinduism: "This is the sum of duty: do not do to others what would cause pain if done to you." (Mahabharata, 5:1517)

Islam: "Not one of you truly believes until you wish for others what you wish for yourself." (The Prophet Muhammad, Hadith)

Jainism: "One should treat all the creatures in the world as one would like to be treated." (Mahavira, Sutrakritanga)

Judaism: "What is hateful to you, do not do to your neighbor. That is the whole Torah; all the rest is commentary." (Hillel, Talmud, Shabbat 31a)

Native American Spirituality: "We are as much alive as we keep the world alive." (Chief Dan George)

Sikhism: "I am a stranger to no one; and no one is a stranger to me. Indeed, I am a friend to all." (Guru Granth Sahib, pg. 1299)

Taoism: "Regard your neighbor's grain as your own grain, and your neighbor's loss as your own loss." (T'ai Shang Kan Ying P'ien, 213–218)

Unitarianism: "We affirm and promote respect for the interdependent web of all existence of which we are a part." (Unitarian Principle)

Zoroastrianism: "Do not unto others whatever is injurious to yourself." (Shayast-na-Shayast, 13.29)

Oh, did I say a "couple examples" of it appear in religions? Sorry. I meant to say that some version of it's taught in just about every freaking major religion there is. And it says a lot, considering how historically divisive religion typically is, that the most fundamental belief of so many of the major religions is basically the same.

Not only is it the same, but it's celebrated in its similarity. I pulled most of the examples above from a poster bragging about this universality. Hell, the name itself is braggadocious: the *Golden* Rule. The one rule to rule them all. What is this? *Lord of the Rings*?

No. This is real life.

WHAT'S WRONG WITH THE GOLDEN RULE?

Let me tell you a story.

I was playing soccer one day when I overheard a spat. It had nothing to do with soccer (a largely drama-free sport), but we were on the field.

"I'm pissed that you made that comment on my picture [on Facebook]," he snapped.

"I didn't realize it'd make you mad," she replied. "That kind of thing never upsets me. It was a joke. Why are you so sensitive?"

The Golden Rule's corruption doesn't even respect the sacred boundaries of a soccer pitch.

You didn't catch it? Oh, sorry. Let's review the play-by-play.

"I didn't realize it'd make you mad."

We often base our assumptions on hypothesizing how someone else might feel, react, etc. in a certain situation. And we all know the danger with assuming and that silly expression I never get right (it does something to our asses?). Some might say it's human nature. It's in our DNA. I don't think that's necessarily the case. But we can all agree, whatever the root, assumptions can be dangerous.

"That kind of thing never upsets me."

Another way we fuel our assumptions is by "putting ourselves in others' shoes" and guesstimating (a word I learned in fifth grade that means "to make up") how they would react. Try as you might, you *cannot* put yourself in someone else's shoes. This statement is the essence of what's wrong with the Golden Rule, so I'll say it again: try as you might, you cannot put yourself in someone else's shoes. "I didn't do unto you as I would not have you do unto me, dude." The "dude" freshens it up a bit, don't you think?

"It was a joke. Why are you so sensitive?"

Ouch. Salt in the wound. What she was really saying was, "Dude (fresh, right?), I did unto you exactly how I would have had you do unto me, yet you are still upset, so clearly there is something wrong with you. What I did was completely justified and reinforced by thousands of iterations of the Golden Rule that have been socialized unto my head recursively since birth, dude."

THE CORRUPTION OF THE GOLDEN RULE

The Golden Rule, despite being based upon what I would assume (oops!) were good intentions, is inherently flawed. Treating others how we want to be treated assumes others want to be treated how we want to be treated, and thusly, that all people want to be treated the same way. Without going any further, you should already have a strong basis for ditching the Golden Rule.

So following the Golden Rule requires us to assume what will make other individuals happy/comfortable/not grumbly and then act on those assumptions in an effort of goodness (bad plan).

But what's worse is that we have been taught and retaught the Golden Rule so many times that we internally justify this method of behavior as invincible, despite the fact that it fails constantly. We believe that our intentions are more important than the outcomes of our actions, because "it's the thought that counts," right? Wrong. You can read more about this in the Chapter 26, but for now just know that it's outcomes that count, not intentions.

Have you ever worked with a "difficult person"? I would bet (not much money because I don't have much money) that those "difficulties" you faced were exacerbated by your (probably) inadvertent exercising of the Golden Rule. Do unto a difficult (=different from you) person as you would have done unto you (=same as you), and you're going to be done unto with a headache and a screaming sound inside your head.

The Golden Rule is as relentless in ruining our happy relationships as it is universal.

So what? Am I just going to tear apart your social foundation of goodness and leave you starving for a way to make those around you happy? Never. I'll feed you.

INTRODUCING: THE PLATINUM RULE

Platinum is worth about three times as much as gold (per ounce, market value). That's important for the name. Keep that in mind. The Platinum Rule is so simple that I'm going to write it twice.

"Do unto others as they would have done unto them, dudes." Again, but with emphasis, that's "Do unto others *as they would have done unto them, dudes.*"

"How do I figure out how other people want to be treated?" I'm always asked in a sassy, know-it-all tone.

"Easy," I slyly reply (good rhyme!). "Ask them."

Ask others how they want to be treated. Ask them how you can be the best (friend, teacher, student, boss, employee, child, parent, etc.) possible, based on their needs and wants.

Ask them how you should support them when they are down, and how you can help them celebrate when they are up. Learn what frustrates them and avoid that. Learn what helps them deal with frustrations they are experiencing and foster that.

Ask them how you can be a good person to them, the kind of person you've always wanted to be while you were following the Golden Rule but so often fell a bit short of.

It can't be that simple, can it?

Oh, it can. And it is.

The basis of the Platinum Rule is similar to the basis of the Golden Rule: above all else, attempt to do no harm. But the unfortunate flaw of the Golden Rule is that the more strictly you follow it, the more inevitably it leads you to doing harm by accident.

The Platinum Rule is also based on this "do no harm" philosophy, but following it provides you with the means to actually do no harm. And even better, the Platinum Rule goes a step further, from proscribing you from harming others to prescribing you to do the best you can to see to others' needs.

Avoiding harm is great, but seeking out opportunities to provide support and foster happiness is even greater.

A FINAL NOTE: THE PLATINUM RULE AND THIS BOOK

The Platinum Rule is my life philosophy. I truly believe in its ability to improve the quality of life for all those who practice it, and it underlies everything I write about in this book.

When making recommendations and talking about entire groups of people (like "trans* people," for example), I do my best to present the best way to handle situations most of the time (i.e., fifty-one times out of a hundred). But for every rule, there are exceptions, and when it comes to discussing and understanding identity, there are far more exceptions than there are rules.

With all this considered, every recommendation I make in this book (e.g., "intersex people don't like being labeled as 'hermaphrodites'") is superseded by the Platinum Rule (e.g., if an intersex person tells you they identify with the label "hermaphrodite," that is their right to do so, and you'll serve them best by using that label).

It's helpful to learn general ideas of how you can be inclusive of different groups of people and understand a group in a broad sense, but whenever you can, you should treat individuals on an individual basis.

YOUSOUP Recipe

Ingredients:

base & broth
- race
- ethnicity
- gender
- sexuality
- disability status

early additions
- socioeconomic status
- geographic location
- education
- family structure

optional
- hobbies & passions
- religion & faith
- career
- political beliefs

secret ingredients
- personal experiences
- changes to other ingredients
- hidden identities
- misperception of ingredients

Procedure:

Combine base ingredients to create broth and bring to a boil. Add early additions and simmer over low heat for 18 - 25 years, adding optional and secret ingredients to taste. Makes one You.

CHAPTER 6

UNDERSTANDING INTERSECTIONS OF IDENTITY

HUMAN TRAGEDIES: WE ALL WANT TO BE EXTRAORDINARY AND WE ALL JUST WANT TO FIT IN. UNFORTUNATELY, EXTRAORDINARY PEOPLE RARELY FIT IN.

—Sebastyne Young

In doing the work I do, I often find myself struggling to help people make sense of the two extremes of identity: on one side we have the idea that people in a group are all the same (stereotypes), while the other side supports this idea that everyone is absolutely unique (snowflakes).

I find myself saying, "We're not the same, but we're also not that different," to the furrowing of brows, so I wanted to take a moment here to talk about the relationship between individual identity and social group memberships, as well as introduce a new graphic concept.

This chapter will help you reconcile a lot of what I'll talk about later, specifically the recurring theme of the relationships between individuality, gender norms, gender roles, and gender identity.

THE SNOWFLAKE VS. THE STEREOTYPE

You have been told all your life that you're unique, special, like a snowflake. Nobody is like you. You're one in seven billion (or one in 108 billion, an estimated total number of humans ever, if you want to get technical), and nobody can take that away from you.

Yet at the same time, you've been told that you can guess that someone else will be like everyone else in a particular group based on their membership in that group (e.g., a gay person will be like gay people). And in your life you've seen evidence that supports this idea.

So which is true?

Both. Kinda.

You're Part Snowflake

You, at a basic level, are a combination of dozens (or more) of identities that merge to form one unique individual. Some of these identities were granted to you at birth (e.g., race, ethnicity, gender, sexuality), others were imposed on or ascribed to you as a child (e.g., socioeconomic status, geographical location, education), some are your choice throughout life (e.g., religion, hobbies, career) and some aren't (e.g., disability status, identities falsely assumed of you by others).

Take all of your identities, add them up, and you get you. There has likely never been another person, in all the 108 billion of Earth's history, whose You Soup recipe was identical to yours. Deeeelish.

But You're Part Stereotype

Calm down, Snowflake. Gimme a second here. Remember all those identities I talked about before? Each one has a long list of stereotypes attached to it—expectations we make of people based on their group identities. This affects you in two distinct ways.

One, in situations where one of those identities is salient (a fancy word we use to mean "particularly prominent"), folks will tend to ascribe the stereotypes of that identity to you, whether you're expressing them or not, or may be hypersensitive to anything you might do to reinforce those stereotypes. And if people see you as a stereotypical X, they will treat you like a stereotypical X.

Two, many of us unknowingly act out stereotypes of group identities we possess or are drawn (knowingly or subconsciously) to particular groups based on certain stereotypes. Further, some folks act in stereotypical ways when figuring out their identity because they feel like they should (this is called internalizing oppression).

So as much as you know you're a fully unique You Soup, in many situations throughout your life you will only be seen as one or two commonplace ingredients (rhubarb if you're lucky, because that one's fun to say).

Why This Doesn't Rock

You know you're not one ingredient; you're a unique flavor that could only be created by a combination of all of your ingredients, in exactly the right proportions (which, if you're Paula Dean, would be a proportion of 2:1, butter to everything else). Yet many times in your life you're going to be viewed as a one-ingredient dish.

You also know that other people are just as unique, yet whether you realize it or not, you're constantly seeing them as one-ingredient concoctions as well, and if that one ingredient is one you've heard nothing but bad things about, you'll probably never even taste them and learn their true flavor. OK. This analogy is getting gross.

Why This Rocks

As you start forcing yourself to realize that everyone is made up of dozens and dozens of different ingredients, many of which make up a part of your You Soup, you'll realize something reality-shaking: even though you're completely unique, you're really *not* unique (you're a unique combination of common ingredients), and that can be awesome.

It's rocks to know that every person you meet probably shares at least one aspect identity with you, a form of common ground. It's comforting to know that there are other people out there who know your plight or have shared in your experiences. In this way, these big-picture group identities are wonderful to have.

THINGS TO MULL OVER

OK. So you understand the idea of You Soup, and you have a better idea of how we can be absolutely unique and not absolutely unique, all at the same time. Here's some food for thought as you continue to chew on this idea. OK. Yes, I'm a little addicted to this analogy:

Even though you may share a group identity with someone, you don't necessarily know their story. Ever noticed how some foods taste better with other foods in the same bite (like how cheese makes broccoli edible?). Identities are the same way: the combinations make a huge difference.

Even though you may share a group identity with someone, you don't necessarily know their story. Sorry. This is incredibly important, so I felt I had to say it twice.

Be careful deconstructing a person (even yourself) down to the individual ingredients. While this will be a great learning experience and eye-opening in many ways, for every ingredient you know about, there is likely one you don't (this goes for you, but more so for others), and those secret ingredients might have the biggest impact of all.

Try to have a relationship with an entire person, not with one of their identities. You are inevitably going to be drawn to certain ingredients in others, but a healthier relationship is one that is holistically inclusive of all identities.

CHAPTER 7

CHECKING YOUR PRIVILEGE

WHAT IS A MINORITY? THE CHOSEN HEROES OF THIS EARTH HAVE BEEN IN A MINORITY.
THERE IS NOT A SOCIAL, POLITICAL, OR RELIGIOUS PRIVILEGE THAT YOU ENJOY TODAY
THAT WAS NOT BOUGHT FOR YOU BY THE BLOOD AND TEARS AND PATIENT SUFFERING
OF THE MINORITY. IT IS THE MINORITY THAT HAVE STOOD IN THE VAN OF EVERY MORAL
CONFLICT, AND ACHIEVED ALL THAT IS NOBLE IN THE HISTORY OF THE WORLD.

—*John B. Gough*

Privilege is a term we use to describe any unearned advantages you have in society as a result of your identity group memberships. Privilege is not something you choose to receive or dismiss. It is automatically granted to you based on your identity, and it informs the ways individuals and groups interact with and view you.

Privilege is an artifact of oppression, and groups that hold power in the oppression differential typically possess the most privilege. In order to work against oppression, we need to work against our own inherent privilege.

While we cannot "turn off" our privilege, we can "check" our privilege, meaning we can examine and address the privileges that our identities are granted. Checking your privilege makes you more aware of the privilege while putting you in positions where you can make efforts to neutralize your privilege and level the playing field for members of all identity groups (in everything from informal social settings to formal occupational settings).

The first step to checking your privilege is simply gaining cognizance of the privilege attached to your various identity group memberships. In the early '90s, Peggy McIntosh conceived a simple and effective way of doing this that is now commonly referred to as a "privilege checklist."

THE PRIVILEGE CHECKLIST

In a short 1990 essay "White Privilege: Unpacking the Invisible Knapsack," Peggy introduced the idea that people who are white are always carrying with them an "invisible knapsack" filled with resources, guides, maps, blank checks, and other helpful tools that make life easier for them. And further, the idea that members of different races are born with different knapsacks, or sets of tools, they have at their disposal.

She "unpacked" her own knapsack by writing what became the first example of a privilege checklist. In it, she addressed roughly fifty ways she experiences unearned social advantages on a daily basis because of her whiteness.

Expanding on her work, following you will find a few lists I've written that share the contents of several other identity groups' invisible knapsacks. The goal in creating these lists is not to shame members of privileged groups but rather to make cognizant in their minds the privileges with which they were born in hopes of increasing their ability to empathize with individuals who were not so fortunate.

It's worth noting that, as with everything in identity, all of the items on each of these lists apply broadly to the identity groups and are the privileges they typically experience. It is by no means meant to say that every individual within each of these groups will experience every privilege, or experience it in the same way. Intersections of identity play a large role in privilege, as a particularly underprivileged identity a person possesses may cancel out the privileges of another identity they possess.

CISGENDER PRIVILEGE

Following is a list of cisgender identity privileges. If you're not already familiar with the term, "cisgender" means having a biological sex that matches your gender identity and expression, resulting in other people accurately perceiving your gender. If you are cisgender, listed below are benefits that result from your alignment of identity and perceived identity. If you identify as cisgender, there's a good chance you've never thought about these things. Try and be more cognizant, and you'll start to realize how much work we have to do in order to make things better for the transgender folks who don't have access to these privileges. (If you're unsure of what it means to be "transgender," don't worry—you have a whole book ahead of you to figure it out.)

1. You can use public restrooms without fear of verbal abuse, physical intimidation, or arrest.

2. You can use public facilities such as gym locker rooms and store changing rooms without stares, fear, or anxiety.

3. Strangers don't assume they can ask you what your genitals look like and how you have sex.

4. Your validity as a man/woman/human is not based on how much surgery you've had or how well you "pass" as non-transgender.

5. You can walk through the world and generally blend in, not being constantly stared or gawked at, whispered about, pointed at, or laughed at because of your gender expression.

6. You can access gender-exclusive spaces such as the Michigan Womyn's Music Festival, Greek Life, or Take Back the Night and not be excluded due to your trans* status.

7. Strangers call you by the name you provide and don't ask what your "real name" (birth name) is and then assume that they have a right to call you by that name.

8. You can reasonably assume that your ability to acquire a job, rent an apartment, or secure a loan will not be denied on the basis of your gender identity/expression.

9. You can flirt, engage in courtship, or form a relationship and not fear that your biological status may be cause for rejection or attack, nor will it cause your partner to question their sexual

orientation.

10. If you end up in the emergency room, you do not have to worry that your gender will keep you from receiving appropriate treatment or that all of your medical issues will be seen as a result of your gender.

11. Your identity is not considered a mental pathology ("gender identity disorder" in the DSM IV) by the psychological and medical establishments.

12. You have freedom from worry about being placed in a sex-segregated detention center, holding facility, jail, or prison that is incongruent with your identity.

13. You have freedom from being profiled on the street as a sex worker because of your gender expression.

14. You are not required to undergo an extensive psychological evaluation in order to receive basic medical care.

15. You do not have to defend you right to be a part of "Queer" (or the queer community), and gays and lesbians will not try to exclude you from "their" equal rights movement because of your gender identity (or any equality movement, including feminist rights).

16. If you are murdered (or have any crime committed against you), your gender expression will not be used as a justification for your murder ("gay panic") nor as a reason to coddle the perpetrators.

17. You can easily find role models and mentors to emulate who share your identity.

18. Hollywood accurately depicts people of your gender in films and television, and does not solely make your identity the focus of a dramatic storyline or the punch line of a joke.

19. You can assume that everyone you encounter will understand your identity and will not think you're confused, misled, or hell-bound when you reveal it to them.

20. You can purchase clothes that match your gender identity without being refused service, mocked by staff, or questioned about your genitals.

21. You can purchase shoes that fit your gender expression without having to order them in special sizes or asking someone to custom-make them.

22. No stranger checking your identification or driver's license will ever insult or glare at you because your name or sex does not match the sex they believed you to be based on your gender expression.

23. You can reasonably assume that you will not be denied services at a hospital, bank, or other institution because the staff does not believe the gender marker on your ID card to match your gender identity.

24. Your gender is an option on a form.

25. You can tick a box on a form without someone disagreeing and telling you not to lie.

26. You don't have to fear interactions with police officers due to your gender identity.

27. You can go places with friends on a whim knowing there will be bathrooms there you can use.

28. You don't have to convince your parents of your true gender and/or have to earn your parents' and siblings' love and respect all over again because of your gender identity.

29. You don't have to remind your extended family over and over to use proper gender pronouns (e.g., after transitioning).

30. You don't have to deal with old photographs that do not reflect who you truly are.

31. If you're dating someone, you know they aren't just looking to satisfy a curiosity or kink pertaining to your gender identity (e.g., the "novelty" of having sex with a trans* person).

32. You can pretend that anatomy and gender are irrevocably entwined when having the "boy parts and girl parts" talk with children, instead of having to explain the actual complexity of the issue.

MALE PRIVILEGE

Following is a list of male privileges. If you are male (and a man), listed below are benefits that result from being born with that gender and sex. If you identify as a man, there's a good chance you've never thought about these things. Try and be more cognizant of these privileges in your daily life, and you'll understand how much work we have to do to make a society that is equitable to all people, regardless of their sex or gender.

1. If you have a bad day or are in a bad mood, people aren't going to blame it on your sex.

2. You can be careless with your money and not have people blame it on your sex.

3. You can be a careless driver and not have people blame it on your sex.

4. You can be confident that your coworkers won't assume you were hired because of your sex.

5. If you are never promoted, it isn't because of your sex.

6. You can expect to be paid equitably for the work you do and not paid less because of your sex.

7. If you are unable to succeed in your career, that won't be seen as evidence against your sex in the workplace.

8. A decision to hire you won't be based on whether the employer assumes you will be having children in the near future.

9. You can generally work comfortably (or walk down a public street) without the fear of sexual harassment.

10. You can generally walk alone at night without the fear of being raped or otherwise harmed.

11. You can go on a date with a stranger without the fear of being raped.

12. You can dress how you want and not worry it will be used as a defense if you are raped.

13. If you are straight, you are not likely to be abused by your partner or be told to continue living in an abusive household for your children.

14. You can decide not to have children and not have your masculinity questioned.

15. If you choose to have children, you will be praised for caring for your children instead of being expected to be the full-time caretaker.

16. You can balance a career and a family without being called selfish for not staying at home (or being constantly pressured to stay at home).

17. If you are straight and decide to have children with your partner, you can assume this will not affect your career.

18. If you rise to prominence in an organization/role, no one will assume it is because you slept your way to the top.

19. You can seek political office without having your sex be a part of your platform.

20. You can seek political office without fear of your relationship with your children, or who you hire to take care of them, being scrutinized by the press.

21. Most political representatives share your sex, particularly the higher-ups.

22. Your political officials fight for issues that pertain to your sex.

23. You can ask for the "person in charge" and will likely be greeted by a member of your sex.

24. As a child, you were able to find plenty of nonlimiting, gender-role-stereotyped media to view.

25. You can disregard your appearance without worrying about being criticized at work or in social situations.

26. You can spend time on your appearance without being criticized for upholding unhealthy gender norms.

27. If you're not conventionally attractive (or in shape), you don't have to worry as much about that negatively affecting your social or career potential.

28. You are not pressured by peers and society to be thin as much as the opposite sex.

29. You're not expected to spend excessive amounts of money on grooming, style, and appearance to fit in while making less money than the opposite sex.

30. You can have promiscuous sex and be viewed positively for it.

31. You can go to a car dealership or mechanic and assume you'll get a fair deal and not be taken advantage of.

32. Expressions and conventional language reflect your sex (e.g., mailman, "all men are created equal").

33. Every major religion in the world is led by individuals of your sex.

34. You can practice religion without subjugating yourself or thinking of yourself as less because of your sex.

35. You are less likely to be interrupted in conversation than members of the opposite sex.

HETEROSEXUAL PRIVILEGE

Following is a list of examples of heterosexual privilege. If you are straight (or in some cases, perceived to be), you can live without ever having to think twice, face, confront, engage, or cope with anything listed below. These privileges are granted to you simply for being born straight, and many of them are things you've likely taken for granted.

1. Being granted immediate access to your loved one in case of accident or emergency.

2. Receiving public recognition and support for an intimate relationship (e.g., congratulations for an engagement).

3. Expressing affection in most social situations and not expecting hostile or violent reactions from others.

4. Living with your partner openly.

5. Expressing pain when a relationship ends from death or separation and receiving support from others.

6. Receiving social acceptance from neighbors, colleagues, and good friends.

7. Learning about romance and relationships from fictional movies and television shows.

8. Having role models of your gender and sexual orientation.

9. Having positive and accurate media images of people with whom you can identify.

10. Expecting to be around others of your sexuality most of the time. Not worrying about being the only one of your sexuality in a class, on a job, or in a social situation.

11. Talking openly about your relationship, vacations, and family planning you and your lover/partner are doing.

12. Easily finding a neighborhood in which residents will accept how you have constituted your household.

13. Raising, adopting, and teaching children without people believing that you will molest them or force them into your sexuality.

14. Working in a traditionally male- or female-dominated job and not feeling as though you are a representative of your sexuality.

15. Receiving paid leave from employment when grieving the death of your spouse.

16. Assuming strangers won't ask, "How does sex work for you?" or other too-personal questions.

17. Sharing health, auto, and homeowners' insurance policies at reduced rates.

18. Not having to hide or lie about women- or men-only social activities.

19. Acting, dressing, or talking as you choose without it being a reflection on people of your sexuality.

20. Freely teaching about lesbians, gay men, and bisexuals without being seen as having a bias because of your sexuality or forcing your "homosexual agenda" on students.

21. Having property laws work in your favor, filing joint tax returns, and inheriting from your spouse automatically under probate laws.

22. Sharing joint child custody.

23. Going wherever you wish knowing that you will not be harassed, beaten, or killed because of your sexuality.

24. Not worrying about being mistreated by the police or victimized by the criminal justice system because of your sexuality.

25. Legally marrying the person you love.

26. Knowing that your basic civil rights will not be denied or outlawed because some people disapprove of your sexuality.

27. Expecting that your children will be given texts in school that support your kind of family unit and will not be taught that your sexuality is a "perversion."

28. Freely expressing your sexuality without fear of being prosecuted for breaking the law.

29. Belonging to the religious denomination of your choice and

knowing that your sexuality will not be denounced by its religious leaders.

30. Knowing that you will not be fired from a job or denied a promotion based on your sexuality.

31. Not being asked by your child's school to only send one parent to back-to-school night so as not to upset the other parents by having two same-sex partners in the class together.

32. Playing a professional sport and not worrying that your athletic ability will be overshadowed by your sexuality and the fact that you share a locker room with the same gender.

33. Not having to worry about being evicted if your landlord finds out about your sexuality.

34. Not having to "come out" (explain to people that you're straight, as they will most likely assume it).

35. Knowing that people aren't going to mutter about your sexuality behind your back.

36. Knowing that being open with your sexuality isn't going to change how people view you.

37. Being able to live anywhere in the world and find people like yourself, unlike gay people, who are limited geographically. Even if the people in more rural areas aren't homophobic, living in a low-density population means social isolation, lack of a dating pool, etc., for queer folks. Even among urban areas, there're only a few cities in the world, relatively speaking, where gay people can live openly and without too much fear.

38. Being able to have your partner from a different country obtain citizenship in your country through marriage.

39. Not having people think your sexuality is a mental health issue.

40. Not having to think about whether your kid's friend's parents will flip out when they pick their kid up from a play date and are greeted by you and your partner.

41. Not having to worry that people won't let their children play with your children because of your sexuality.

42. Not having to worry about where you can move, alone or with your spouse, and have equal job opportunities abroad.

43. Being able to move abroad with your children without sudden changes of your legal status and the possibly of even losing your children.

CHECKING THE REST OF YOUR PRIVILEGE

The above are only a few examples of privileged identities. There is a good chance you possess other identities that are granted some level of privilege in society (e.g., based on race, ethnicity, disability status, religion, social class).

Take some time to write lists like these for the various identities you possess. It may seem overwhelming, but it's actually frighteningly easy once you get going. Just start with "As a member of _____ group, I have unique access to..." and go from there. This is one of the most important exercises you can partake in when it comes to understanding and advocating for social justice, so dedicate some time to it before moving on.

BREAKING THROUGH THE BINARY

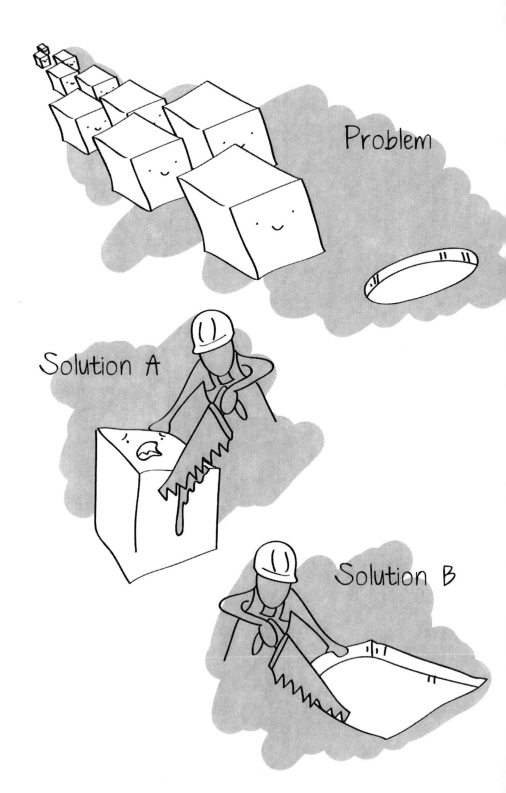

CHAPTER 8

GENDER NORMS

I HAVE NOT LIVED AS A WOMAN. I HAVE LIVED AS A MAN. I'VE JUST
DONE WHAT I DAMN WELL WANTED TO, AND I'VE MADE ENOUGH
MONEY TO SUPPORT MYSELF, AND [I] AIN'T AFRAID OF BEING ALONE.

—*Katharine Hepburn*

When studying gender, three distinct fields of science interplay with one another: psychology, sociology, and biology. This is as fascinating as it is potentially confusing, particularly if you don't have much background in these three areas.

My education and perspective have led me to approach gender (and most of social justice) with a heavy sociological slant, so you'll see sociological themes most prevalent throughout this book. One of the most fundamental ideas in sociology is that of social norms.

Let's talk about social norms in general and then discuss their effect on gender.

SOCIAL NORMS

The down-and-dirty explanation of social norms is that they are informal (usually) rules that a society reinforces and members of that society live by. Sociologists and psychologists have slightly varied takes on this, but the overall idea is the same.

A few examples of social norms: chewing with your mouth closed (and just about anything else you'd group under the umbrellas of "politeness" or "courtesy"); wearing conventional clothing for a particular situation (no PJs at the opera, no tuxedos or dresses to bed); and, a particularly famous one, facing the doors in an elevator and keeping chitchat to a minimum.

While most norms are only informally reinforced (i.e., they aren't illegal), you will often find that the pressure to conform to them is far greater than the pressure to conform to some formally reinforced laws (like jaywalking).

DRILL: Go find an elevator—right now, or rather, after you finish reading this paragraph—and ride it up and down a few times. First, ride it the normal way: facing the doors, mostly silent. See how that feels; take note of your internal dialogue and how you perceive your elevating peers' attitudes toward you. Then, and this is the fun (horrible) part, do the exact opposite: stand with your back to the door at the front of the elevator, facing your soon-to-be elevating friends (enemies), make solid eye contact, and engage in serious conversations with them (e.g., introduce yourself, ask them why they are riding the elevator, what they are doing with their lives, what their social security numbers are—ya know, normal stuff). Now take note of your feelings and what you perceive their attitudes toward you to be.

What's fascinating about social norms is how powerful their influence can be. Take the example of incorrectly riding an elevator compared to the example of jaywalking.

We are never taught how to ride elevators. There are no signs, rulebooks, or other formal indicators that inform us what the correct way to ride in an elevator is. However, even without that, we could each individually write down a list of "rules of elevator riding" and they would be remarkably similar. The process through which we learned those rules is called socialization.

Now let's consider jaywalking. Jaywalking is a formal crime complete with indicators from signs on the street and written laws in law books, and our government and our parents formally teach us that it is unacceptable behavior. There is even a serious repercussion (if you're not rollin' in the dollas) if you choose to break this rule and are caught.

But if you were to break the jaywalking rule (legal note: this publication does not condone reckless abandon of the law even for the express purpose of social experimentation—*kidding, freak what you feel*), and then break the elevator riding rule, Vegas odds go to the second experience feeling far more wrong. Why is this?

Social norms often trump formal laws when it comes to pre-scribing acceptable behavior. And in this particular case, it just so happens that engaging in jaywalking is a social norm (i.e., it is something we as a society encourage, or at least condone). What a crazy, mixed-up, hypocritical society we live in, where formal laws are often felt less severely than informal laws and our informal laws often directly conflict with formal laws.

And we're just getting started.

SOCIAL NORMS + GENDER = GENDER NORMS

Keeping everything I just presented in mind, let's focus on a particular subset of social norms: gender norms. Just about everything in this book is based on gender norms, so it's probably worth giving them a once-over.

Like all social norms, gender norms are informal rules that our society imposes on us and that we feel an immense amount of pressure to follow. But unlike a lot of social norms, gender norms are often formally taught to us, and the consequences for following or breaking them can be equally dire, depending on your individual identity (I'll come back to this, so don't worry if you don't follow right now).

And also unlike most social norms, gender norms are so pervasive in our society that they are inescapable. No matter what you are doing, where you are, who you are with, or what time of day it is—even when you're asleep—you're being influenced by a gender norm (or a few hundred).

GENDER NORMS VS. GENDER ROLES

A "role" is a societal station or position with a list of prescribed behaviors and responsibilities. An example of a role we're all likely familiar with is worker. Like with norms, occupiers of roles are informally pressured to behave in certain ways or possess certain characteristics (e.g., workers should be timely, be appropriately dressed, put their employers' needs before their own, etc.). Or, put another way, every role comes with a specific set of norms.

The difference between gender norms and gender roles, then, is that gender norms are informal laws of society pertaining to gender, while gender roles are specific groupings of those gender norms that result in specific societal positions. Think of gender norms as ingredients (tomatoes, onions, avocados, salt, pepper, lime, cilantro) and gender roles as finished dishes (guacamole, or should I say guacamanle? OK. I guess I shouldn't have).

DRILL: Take five minutes and write down as many gender norms as you can. Go as fast as you can, don't overthink it, don't consider what's "right" or "wrong"—just write down everything that pops into your mind and see how many you can come up with.

A SQUARE SOCIAL ROLE FOR A CIRCLE SOCIETY

Unlike most social roles, adhering to sets of gender norms (gender roles) can create as much dissonance for some folks as breaking them. That is, there are millions of people for whom gender roles create a no-win situation: breaking them creates external conflict, but following them creates conflict within.

This is because unlike other social roles, gender roles tend to overlap and intersect and form one fluid, multifaceted role, instead of several independent roles. How about a concrete example of what I mean?

Consider the following social roles: worker, teacher, student, boss, father, mother, son, daughter. The first four could be considered genderless social roles (even though this isn't entirely true, let's just go with that for the sake of time), while the latter four are gendered.

The first four roles could be filled by one person, all in the course of the day, without any issues. This happens in many workplaces every day. Take my previous career of university administrator for example. All day I was an employee of the university who followed all the inherent worker norms (e.g., I dressed professionally, showed up on time, worked hard all day, was polite and helpful whenever I could be, etc.) in order to be viewed in a positive light; I would often be called on to be a teacher for a colleague (generally this involved helping someone with something computery); similarly, I was constantly learning new things from my colleagues (i.e., being a student); and I supervised student groups, occupying the boss role for them.

No issues there, right? Right. Now, let's consider the latter four roles, the gendered ones, from my list above: father, mother, son, daughter.

In an attempt to fill all four of these social roles in one day in my interactions with those around me, I would likely end up, at the least, alarming everyone. And I am surrounded by an understanding group of friends and family who expect "abnormal" behavior from me. For many people this type of behavior would result in much more severe social repercussions.

Why can I not be all those roles (or really any of them but one)? Because the gendered roles I'm allowed to play are ascribed to me based on the gender those around me ascribe to me. Think of life as a play with limited roles to fill and every time you interact with someone else as an audition, with them considering your audition and casting you for a part in the play.

But instead of being cast as a Montague or a Capulet, you're cast as a Man or a Woman. And even if you're not prepared for one of those parts (you don't know the lines, you can't fit into the tights, you're afraid of heights and don't like balconies), you're going to play it anyhow because those are your options, and you're going onstage whether you want to or not.

IS IT THE GOAL OF THIS BOOK TO "BREAK" GENDER NORMS?

No. In fact, it's possible for gender norms to be a generally supportive and healthy component of a society, to contribute to ideas that are important for understanding our own and other people's genders, and eventually work toward a goal of gender equity.

"Whaaaaa?" you might be thinking. Don't worry. There's a small part of me screaming that, too. Give me a second to try to make you and me feel a bit better with this before we move on, Gender Warrior. And remember, "Wars not make one great."

While gender norms (and particularly the roles that spawn from them) can be incredibly restrictive, norms also create a common language with which we can discuss and explore gender, our own identities, and those of others. Gender norms also provide a lot of comfort for individuals in that they provide them with the ability to feel as if they are a member of a group with which they identify—a group filled with other people experiencing similar struggles and successes.

The goal of this book is to help you separate the idea of gender from gender roles and to help us move toward a society that allows individuals to embody their gender, the unique mixtures of all the gender ingredients available to them, in whatever way that may be, instead of taking a few of their most obvious traits and forcing that person into a role they weren't born to play.

USING GENDER NORMS CONSTRUCTIVELY

Throughout this book, I'll refer a lot to gender norms as we explain gender identity and diversity. In the Genderbread Person, my model for depicting gender, I rely heavily on gender norms. I break gender into three key aspects with each aspect split into degrees of normalized characteristics (woman-ness/man-ness, maleness/femaleness, and femininity/masculinity—more on all these later). It makes me uncomfortable to do this, but it's necessary discomfort.

It's important that you realize I advocate for these terms in understanding gender solely for the commonality of language they provide. If I say masculine, you have an immediate idea of what that means to you, how you've been socialized to understand masculinity, and it is likely extremely similar to the idea of what it means to me and others around you. This is incredibly helpful.

It's also important that you realize that what masculine means to us may not be the same as what it means to someone who was not socialized in the same ways as us. Folks from different age groups, different regions of the United States, and different countries—just to name a few social groups—are socialized in unique ways. So while using these norms provides the closest thing to a commonality of language, it's by no means universality of language.

So let's tread lightly when employing gender norms, and be sure to keep in mind there is no skeleton key when it comes to understanding any aspect of human identity, particularly not something so complex and near-universally misunderstood as gender.

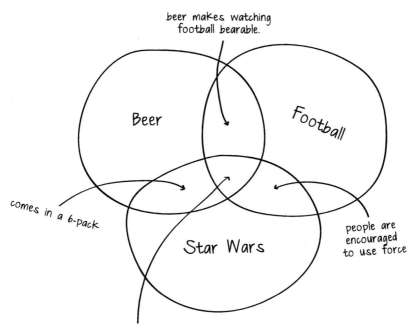

beer makes watching football bearable.

Beer

Football

comes in a 6-pack

Star Wars

people are encouraged to use force

Things men complain that women don't enjoy, while men simultaneously reinforce gender norms that prohibit women from being able to enjoy them without threatening man-ness.

CHAPTER 9

INTRODUCTION TO THE GENDERBREAD PERSON

LIKE MOST QUALITIES, CUTENESS IS DELINEATED BY WHAT IT ISN'T. MOST PEOPLE AREN'T CUTE AT ALL, OR IF SO THEY QUICKLY OUTGROW THEIR CUTENESS... ELEGANCE, GRACE, DELICACY, BEAUTY, AND A LACK OF SELF-CONSCIOUSNESS: A CREATURE WHO KNOWS HE IS CUTE SOON ISN'T.

—*William S. Burroughs*

The Genderbread Person is a simple, accessible, adorable way of demonstrating gender diversity. It is, without question, the most popular doodle I've ever doodled. In the first six months, the Genderbread Person garnered over 80 million views (some on my website, many more via social media sharing and reposting) and was seen in 120 countries and translated into at least six languages. I stopped keeping track of it at that point, but it hasn't gotten any less popular on my site in the past few years.

The idea for the first version of the Genderbread Person has been floating around for many years. The schema used in the oldest version, the four bidirectional continua, has been used in social justice trainings since long before I went to college. And there are even some examples of folks using cookies and other fun foods and ideas as a metaphor for the different aspects of gender. A reader once even wrote to me about a "gender gumby" from her childhood.

My goal in creating the first Genderbread Person was to combine the best available gender schema with an adorable and easy-to-grasp aesthetic. I used a schema that was tried and true because I wanted to do my best not to misinform (that happens too often already); I made it adorable because I wanted it to be inviting and share-worthy; and above all, I wanted to present it in a way that didn't require any experience in gender studies to understand.

It was my hope that with a mere glance, folks would be able to learn the most important thing about gender: quite simply, that what we've all been taught growing up is, at best, incomplete.

Anything beyond that was bonus.

A few minutes past that first glance, folks were able to better understand the ways in which what they were taught was incomplete. It would provoke internal dialogue as well as external dialogue and be a first step in a long process of unpacking misconceptions and starting to get a truer sense of one's self and others.

With the original goal of the graphic accomplished, I began receiving hundreds of e-mails and comments that the graphic wasn't inclusive of all genders and was, in many ways, reinforcing the traditional view of gender that it was meant to reject. Basically, folks were looking for a master's level Genderbread Person, and the one I'd given them was barely a college sophomore.

Not one to walk away from a challenge, I got to work.

The way that I was taught about gender diversity oh so many years ago was based on the schema I used to create the first Genderbread Person. And just as it's difficult to think about gender as anything other than "male and female" if that's what you've been taught your whole life, it can be as difficult to think beyond a system you've been relying on your entire adult life—even a more advanced, inclusive one, such as the first Genderbread Person.

I had to unpack everything I thought I knew about gender the first time I learned it, back when I was at the stage where the original Genderbread Person would have blown my (freakin') mind. Further, I had to start unpacking everything I thought I knew about teaching gender.

That's a lot of unpacking.

To do this, I opened up a dialogue with hundreds of people, ranging the gamut of gender identities and levels of experience with gender issues. For a few weeks I asked and listened, asked and listened, and asked and listened some more until I thought my head was going to pop. Then I started to synthesize what I'd heard and try to make sense of it all.

I reached a point of understanding where I knew what I had to accomplish with the new model and what the range of identities was I needed to represent, but I couldn't get it out of my head and onto paper.

Then, thanks to a few cups of coffee and an in-person conversation with a brilliant colleague and comprehensive sex educator, Karen Rayne, we were finally able to come up with a seed of an idea for a new schema. That initial seed grew into what became the second version of the Genderbread Person and is a much better attempt at visualizing and simplifying something as muddy and complicated as human gender.

In this book, I'm including both the original and the improved versions of the Genderbread Person, with full write-ups explaining how to use each. All of the models have their merits, and because of its simplicity, many folks still share version 1 with people new to understanding gender.

The Genderbread Person is certainly far from perfect. With this book I am releasing a version 3, and hopefully someday soon I'll come up with a version 4 that makes as much of an improvement over 3 as 3 did over 2 and 2 did over 1. No matter what version of the Genderbread Person you use, it is nonetheless a great starting point for learning about gender.

Now if only I can come up with a sensible way to organize my sock drawer.

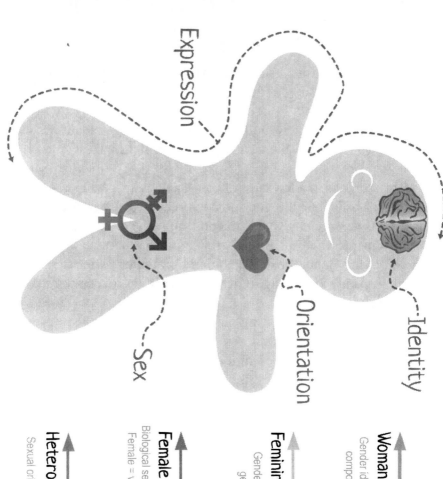

Expression

Identity

Orientation

Sex

 Gender Identity

Woman ←——————————————————→ **Man**

Gender identity is how you, in your head, think about yourself. It's the chemistry that composes you (e.g., hormonal levels) and how you interpret what that means.

 **Gender Expression**

Feminine ←—— **Androgynous** ——→ **Masculine**

Gender expression is how you demonstrate your gender (based on traditional gender roles) through the ways you act, dress, behave, and interact.

Biological Sex

Female ←—— **Intersex** ——→ **Male**

Biological sex refers to the objectively measurable organs, hormones, and chromosomes. Female = vagina, ovaries, XX chromosomes; male = penis, testes, XY chromosomes; intersex = a combination of the two.

 Sexual Orientation

Heterosexual ←—— **Bisexual** ——→ **Homosexual**

Sexual orientation is who you are physically, spiritually, and emotionally attracted to, based on their sex/gender in relation to your own.

CHAPTER 10

USING THE GENDERBREAD PERSON

IF YOU CAN'T EXPLAIN IT TO A SIX-YEAR-OLD, YOU DON'T UNDERSTAND IT YOURSELF.

—Albert Einstein

Gender is a tough subject to tackle. There are many facets to consider and many pressures at play, and we have all been conditioned in such a way that our first instinct is almost unanimously wrong. But we're going to tackle it. No. We're going to tackle the snot out of it. Coming to our aid, I would like to present to you: The Genderbread Person!

Now let's talk about it.

THE GENDERBREAD PERSON

As you'll see above, we have four elements. Before I break them down, I want to talk in generalities. First of all, if you noticed that the first three categories all pertain to gender while the fourth pertains to sexuality, great job. Skip ahead to the next paragraph. For everyone else: if that doesn't make sense to you, or you're unsure of how all four interrelate, worry not. By the end of this chapter, it'll all make sense or you can have your money back. And if you never gave me money, give me money.

Whenever I talk to groups about gender using this model, a common problem arises: people tend to assume that someone will consistently be some degree of either the left half or the right half of each of the top three continuums above (all left, or all right), and when I explain that many people zigzag through the list, they give me blank stares. I'm about to say something that will likely freak you out, but be cool; it'll all make sense soon. Gender identity, gender expression, biological sex, and sexual orientation are independent of one another (i.e., they are not connected). With that said (I'm going to say it again later), let's move on.

🧠 Gender Identity

Woman   Genderqueer   Man

Gender identity is how you, in your head, think about yourself. It's the chemistry that composes you (e.g., hormonal levels) and how you interpret what that means.

GENDER IDENTITY: WHO YOU THINK YOU ARE

On the left we have "woman" and on the right we have "man," two terms you are likely already familiar with. In the middle, we have the term "genderqueer," which, you guessed it, is used for an identity that is somewhere between woman and man. Another term for genderqueer that is accepted within the trans* community is "genderfuck," but that's a bit racy for my taste. It's also important to note that many people consider their identity to fall outside of the traditional (and limited) woman-to-man spectrum. These identities can be called transgender, genderqueer, agender, third-gender, bigender, and more.

Gender identity is all about how you think about yourself. It's about how you internally interpret the physical chemistry that composes as it relates to the socialization you experienced growing up. As you know it, do you think you fit better into the societal role of "woman" or "man," or does neither ring particularly true for you? That is, are you somewhere between the two? Or do you consider your gender to fall outside the spectrum completely? The answers to these questions are what we would define as your gender identity.

It has been accepted that we form our gender identities around the age of three and that after that age, it is incredibly difficult to change them. Formation of gender identity is affected by hormones and environment just as much as it is by biological sex. Oftentimes, problems arise when someone is assigned a gender based on their sex at birth that doesn't align with how they come to identify. We'll talk about that more later.

Feminine   Androgynous   Masculine

Gender expression is how you demonstrate your gender (based on traditional gender roles) through the ways you act, dress, behave, and interact.

GENDER EXPRESSION: HOW YOU DEMONSTRATE WHO YOU ARE

On the left we have "feminine," and on the right we have "masculine," the two expressive terms related to "woman" and "man." In the middle, we have a new term, "androgynous," which describes an ambiguous or mixed form of expressing gender.

Gender expression is all about how you demonstrate your gender through the ways you act, dress, behave, and interact—whether that is intentional or unintended. Gender expression is interpreted by others perceiving your gender based on traditional gender roles (e.g., men wear pants; women wear dresses). Gender expression is something that often changes from day to day, outfit to outfit, and event or setting to event or setting. It's about how the way you express yourself aligns or doesn't with traditional ways of gendered expression. And like gender identity, there is a lot of room for flexibility here. It is likely that you slide around on this continuum throughout the week without even thinking about it. How about an example?

You wake up wearing baggy gray sweatpants and a T-shirt. As you walk into your kitchen to prepare breakfast, you're expressing an androgynous-to-slightly masculine gender. However, you see your partner in the kitchen and prowl in like Halle Berry from Catwoman. Then you are expressing much more femininely, so now you're back on the left half of the continuum. You pour a bowl of cereal, wrap your fist around a spoon like a Viking, and start shoveling Fruit

Loops into your face, and all of a sudden you're sliding back onto the right side of the continuum. After breakfast, you skip back into your bedroom and playfully place varying outfits in front of you, pleading with your partner to help you decide what to wear. You're feminine again.

I assume this entire time you were imagining it was you, with your gender identity, acting out that example. Now go back through the whole thing, but this time imagine someone with a different gender identity from you going through the motions. Now you are starting to understand how these concepts interrelate but don't interconnect.

Female   Intersex   Male

Biological sex refers to the objectively measurable organs, hormones, and chromosomes. Female = vagina, ovaries, XX chromosomes; male = penis, testes, XY chromosomes; intersex = a combination of the two.

BIOLOGICAL SEX: THE EQUIPMENT UNDER THE HOOD

On the left we have "female," and on the right we have "male," the two biological sexes we all grew up knowing about. In the middle, we have a new term, "intersex," which describes someone whose sexual organs are not strictly male or female. The term "hermaphrodite," which you've likely heard used to describe an intersex individual, is frowned upon as "hermaphrodite" is a stigmatizing word that means someone who is entirely male and female, a biological impossibility. Oh, and how did you feel about me expressing my masculinity in the heading of this section?

Biological sex refers to the objectively measurable organs, hormones, and chromosomes you possess. Let's consider biological sex in the ultra-reductive way society does: being female means having a vagina, ovaries, two X chromosomes, predominant estrogen, and the ability to grow a baby in your abdominal area; being male means having testes, a penis, an XY chromosome configuration, predominant testosterone, and the ability to put a baby in a female's abdominal area; and being intersex can be any combination of what I just described.

In reality, biological sex, like gender identity and expression, for most folks, is more nuanced than that. We will get to that in a later chapter, but for now I want to talk a bit more about intersex people.

For example, someone can be born with the appearance of being male (penis, scrotum, etc.), but have a functional female reproductive system inside. There are many examples of how intersex can present itself, and below you can see some statistics from the Intersex Society of North America illustrating the frequency of intersex births. (Check out the stat I bolded, but be prepared to be shocked.)

Not XX and Not XY	*1 in 1,666 births*
Klinefelter (XXY)	*1 in 1,000 births*
Androgen Insensitivity Syndrome	*1 in 13,000 births*
Partial Androgen Insensitivity Syndrome	*1 in 130,000 births*
Classical Congenital Adrenal Hyperplasia	*1 in 13,000 births*
Late Onset Adrenal Hyperplasia	*1 in 66 individuals*
Vaginal Agenesis	*1 in 6,000 births*
Ovotestes	*1 in 6,000 births*
Idiopathic (no discernible medical cause)	*1 in 110,000 births*
Iatrogenic (caused by medical treatment)	*no estimate*
5 Alpha Reductase Deficiency	*no estimate*
Mixed Gonadal Dysgenesis	*no estimate*
Complete Gonadal Dysgenesis	*1 in 150,000 births*
Hypospadias (in perineum or penile shaft)	*1 in 2,000 births*
Hypospadias (between corona and tip of penis)	*1 in 770 births*
Total number of people whose bodies differ from standard male or female	**1 in 100 births**
Total number of people receiving surgery to "normalize" genital appearance	*1 or 2 in 1,000 births*

Sexual Orientation

Heterosexual   Bisexual   Homosexual

Sexual orientation is who you are physically, spiritually, and emotionally attracted to, based on their sex/gender in relation to your own.

SEXUAL ORIENTATION: WHO YOU ARE ATTRACTED TO

On the left we have "heterosexual," meaning attracted to people of the opposite gender, or being straight. On the right we have "homosexual," meaning attracted to people of the same gender, or being gay or lesbian. And in the middle we have bisexual, meaning attracted to your gender as well as a different gender. Note: there is no place on the scale for "asexual," which is the lack of sexual attraction to others, as it doesn't fit into this continuum.

Sexual orientation is all about who you are physically, spiritually, and emotionally attracted to. If you are male and you're attracted to females, you're straight. If you're a male who is attracted to males and females, you're bisexual. And if you're a male who is attracted to males, you're gay. This is the one most of us know the most about. We hear the most about it, it's salient in our lives, and we can best understand where we stand with it. It's pretty cut and dry, right? Maybe.

Interestingly enough, pioneering research conducted by Dr. Alfred Kinsey in the mid-twentieth century uncovered that most people aren't absolutely straight or gay/lesbian. Instead of just asking "Do you like dudes or chicks?" (very sciency, I know), he asked people to report their fantasies, dreams, thoughts, emotional investments in others, and frequency of sexual contact. Based on his findings, he broke sexuality down into a seven-point scale (see below) and reported that most people who identify as straight are actually somewhere between 1 and 3 on the scale, and most people who identify as lesbian/gay are between 3 and 5, meaning most of us are a little bi-.

0—Exclusively Heterosexual

1—Predominantly heterosexual, incidentally homosexual

2—Predominantly heterosexual, but more than incidentally homosexual

3—Equally heterosexual and homosexual

4—Predominantly homosexual, but more than incidentally heterosexual

5—Predominantly homosexual, incidentally heterosexual

6—Exclusively Homosexual

PUTTING IT ALL TOGETHER: INTERRELATION VS. INTERCONNECTION

Wow. That was a lot of information all at once, can we agree? The crazy part: I held back. Later in this book are individual chapters on each of the sections above, because there is still so much to say. But you don't need to worry about that right now. We need to make this all make sense—synthesize some knowledge all up in your brain.

Remember earlier when I said that thing and then said I would say it again? This is me saying that again: though the four things I presented above are certainly interrelated, they are not interconnected. What do I mean by that?

Gender identity, gender expression, biological sex, and sexual orientation are independent of one another (i.e., they are not connected). People's sexual orientation doesn't determine their gender expression. And their gender expression isn't determined by their gender identity. And their gender identity isn't determined by their biological sex. And also, every other mismatch of Y isn't determined by Z combination you can dream up from those inputs. Those things certainly affect one another (i.e., they are related to one another), but they do not determine one another.

Knowing where an individual falls on two of the gender continua does not mean you can accurately predict where they will land in the others. This is an erroneous assumption we often make (e.g., that because you know someone identifies as "woman" and expresses femininely she is female). Further, knowing all the aspects of a person's gender does not mean you can predict what their sexual orientation will. For example, "Man, male, feminine means he's gay, right?" Wrong.

However, these things do tend to be socially linked in ways that trick us into thinking they are biologically determined. For example, if someone is born with male reproductive organs and genitalia, he is very likely to be raised as a boy, identify as a man, and express himself masculinely. We call this identity "cisgender" (when your biological sex aligns with how you identify), and it grants a lot of privilege (you already read about that, remember?). It's something most of us don't appreciate nearly as much as we should, if we have it.

CHAPTER II

WHY THE NEW MODEL IS BETTER

ANY CHANGE, EVEN A CHANGE FOR THE BETTER, IS ALWAYS
ACCOMPANIED BY DRAWBACKS AND DISCOMFORTS.

—*Arnold Bennett*

I would really like to see the new model replace all instances of the old Genderbread person because it's more accurate, more inclusive, and still just as accessible (adorable). However, I realize that this model takes a bit more of a leap of understanding for newcomers to the gender identity discussion.

I'm calling the new way of mapping things out the "-Ness" Model (independent unidirectional linear continua model seemed wordy), and it overcomes most of the hiccups of the old Genderbread (continua-based) and other models (2D plots, universe models, matrices, Venn diagrams, etc.) available in the gender education world.

Let me address some of the key reasons I think this new version is better, and you can decide which you'd rather use after it's all said and done.

THE NEW VERSION IS MORE ACCURATE

Men are from Mars and women are from Venus is a funny expression (and scientifically dubious), but it actually nails down the strength of this model: two planets, not two poles of one planet. Placing man/masculine/male on one end of something (continuum, 2D plot, etc.) and woman/feminine/female on the other (as I did with the old model) creates and reinforces a fallacy central to gender misunderstanding: to be more of one, you need to be less of the other. That's incorrect. You can have both. You can have your genderbread and eat it, too.

Let's take "Gender Identity," for example. I identify as a man, but I identify with a lot of what it means to be a woman. I'm sensitive, kind, familial, and I really like dark chocolate (kidding—stuff's disgusting). Possessing this "woman-ness" doesn't make me any less of a man. But it's a large part of my gender identity, and those traits affect my life and influence my decisions as much as (or more than) much of my "man-ness" does.

This model allows one to define their gender in a way that accounts for varying intensities of -ness. Identifying with aspects of femininity doesn't make you less masculine; it makes you more feminine. To understand gender, and in turn create a safer space for people of all genders, we need to realize that feminine and masculine aren't in a tug of war—they're in separate arenas altogether.

IT'S MORE INCLUSIVE

What was lacking in the old Genderbread Person was the ability to define intensities of identification, or the amount of -ness one possesses. And what's lacking in other available models is the ability to define intensity independently for the two major aspects of gender. Our new model comes up spades in both.

Let's take "Attraction" for our example. We know that most people aren't 100 percent straight or gay, and a continuum of gay to straight (think Kinsey) leaves us with bi- in the middle. What about folks who are pansexual? Asexual? Mostly asexual? Hypersexual? None of those identities can be mapped on our old model. Ditto for the other elements of the model and folks who are agender, pangender, two-spirited, and the list goes on.

The amount of -ness is, in many cases, as crucial to one's identity as which -ness they possess. A man who is hypersexually attracted to women and a man who is attracted to women may both identify as "straight," but there is no question that they are two different men.

AND IT IS JUST AS ADORABLE

While I upped the ante on accuracy and inclusivity, I did my best to avoid compromising what was arguably the most effective aspect of the old Genderbread Person: 'e is freakin' adorable! The original genderbread I baked has been gobbled up millions of times, and I attribute the wealth of that interest to the fact that it was easy to understand and visually appealing.

While this one is a bit harder to understand at first glance—mostly due to the fact that I'm using a plotting method I created instead of a standard graph—most people in the test group got it (even "non-mathy" people). So that's good. It's an introduction, after all, and we know how important introductions are.

Gender is one of those things everyone thinks they understand, but most people don't. Like Inception. Gender isn't binary. It's not either/or. In many cases it's both/and. A bit of this, a dash of that. This tasty little guide is meant to be an appetizer for gender understanding. It's okay if you're hungry for more. In fact, that's the idea.

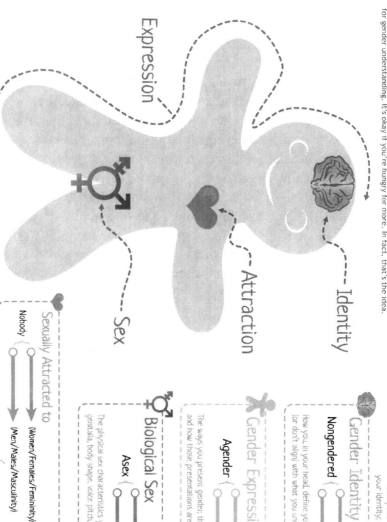

Expression

Identity

Attraction

Sex

Gender Identity

Plot a point on both continua in each category to represent your identity; combine all ingredients to form your Genderbread plot and label combos.

4 (of infinite) possible

Nongendered ——— Woman-ness

——— Man-ness

How you, in your head, define your gender, based on how much you align (or don't align) with what you understand to be the options for gender.

Gender Expression

Agender ——— Feminine

——— Masculine

The ways you present gender, through your actions, dress, and demeanor, and how those presentations are interpreted based on gender norms.

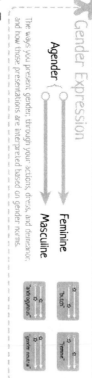

Biological Sex

Asex ——— Female-ness

——— Male-ness

The physical sex characteristics you're born with and develop, including genitalia, body shape, voice pitch, body hair, hormones, chromosomes, etc.

Sexually Attracted to

Nobody ——— (Women/Females/Femininity)

——— (Men/Males/Masculinity)

In each grouping, circle all that apply to you, and plot a point, depicting the aspects of gender toward which you experience attraction

Romantically Attracted to

Nobody ——— (Women/Females/Femininity)

——— (Men/Males/Masculinity)

CHAPTER 12

USING THE NEW GENDERBREAD PERSON

THERE'S NOTHING AS EXCITING AS A COMEBACK—SEEING SOMEONE
WITH DREAMS, WATCHING THEM FAIL, AND THEN GETTING
A SECOND CHANCE.

—*Rachel Griffiths*

As we covered when I introduced the original Genderbread Person, gender is a tough subject to tackle. But we're going to tackle it, and this time, we're going to tackle the balls out of it (How's that for a gendered term?). Coming to our aid, I would like to present to you: The Genderbread Person (version 3)!

The schema used here to map out gender (the "-ness" model) allows individuals to plot where they identify along both continua to represent varying degrees of alignment with the traditional binary elements of each aspect of gender, resulting in infinite possibilities of "gender" for a person.

Also, I strongly condone and recommend people to plot ranges along the continua, instead of just plots, to depict how their gender might vary (as a result of different social stituations, stimulations, or other -ations).

If that was a bit dense for you, it'll all make sense soon. Just know that in each category (gender identity, gender expression, biological sex, and attraction), you are to place a point or range on each of the directional lines representing your man-/ woman-/ masculine-/

feminine-/ male-/ female-ness, whether it be nada or a lotta.

FACT: the "-ness" model I created to attempt to adequate-ly depict the diversity inherent in human gender has been adopted by several university researchers as the model for their ongoing gender studies.

Note: a lot of the language in this chapter is similar to what was in the using the Genderbread Person (version 1) chapter, but modified where necessary for the changes in the new model. I am reprinting it for your ease of reference regardless of what model you choose to embrace. Sorry, Earth.

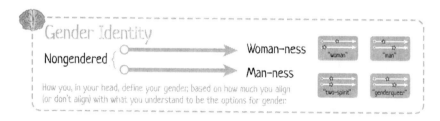

GENDER IDENTITY: WHO YOU THINK YOU ARE

On the left of both continua we have "nongendered," which, you guessed it, means existing without gender, and on the right we have "woman-ness" (the quality to which you identify as a "woman") and "man-ness" (ditto, but with "man"). Below we have some examples of possible plots and possible labels for those plots. Examples of common identities that aren't listed include agender, bigender, third-gender, and transgender.

Gender identity is all about how you think about yourself. It's about how you internally interpret the chemistry that composes you (e.g., hormone levels). As you know it, do you think you fit better into the societal role of "woman" or "man," or does neither ring particularly true for you? That is, do you have aspects of your identity that align with elements from both? Or do you consider your gender to fall outside of the gender norms completely? The answer is your gender identity.

It has been accepted that we form our gender identities around the age of three and that after that age, it is incredibly difficult to change them. Formation of identity is affected by hormones and environment just as much as it is by biological sex. Oftentimes, problems arise when someone is assigned a gender based on their sex at birth that doesn't align with how they come to identify. We'll talk about that more later.

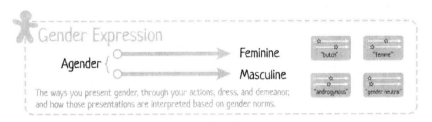

GENDER EXPRESSION: HOW YOU DEMONSTRATE WHO YOU ARE

On the left of both continua we have "agender," which means expression without gender ("genderless"), and on the right sides we have "masculine" and "feminine." Examples of different gender expressions and possible labels are below. "Androgynous" might be a new word, and it simply means a gender expression that has elements of both masculinity and femininity.

Gender expression is all about how you demonstrate gender through the ways you act, dress, behave, and interact—whether that is intentional or unintended. Gender expression is interpreted by others based on traditional gender norms (e.g., men wear pants; women wear dresses). Gender expression is something that often changes from day to day, outfit to outfit, and event or setting to event or setting. It's about how the way you express yourself aligns or doesn't with traditional ways of gendered expression, and can be motivated by your gender identity, sexuality, or something else completely (e.g., just for fun, or performance). Like gender identity, there is a lot of room for flexibility here. It is likely that your gender expression changes frequently without you even thinking about it. How about an example?

You wake up wearing baggy gray sweatpants and a T-shirt. As you walk into your kitchen to prepare breakfast, you're expressing an adrogynous-to-slightly-masculine gender. However, you see your partner in the kitchen and decide to prowl in like Halle Berry from Catwoman, then you are expressing much more femininely. You pour a bowl of cereal, wrap your fist around a spoon like a Viking, and start shoveling Fruit Loops into your face, and all-of-a-sudden you're bumping up your levels of masculinity. After breakfast, you skip back into your bedroom and playfully place varying outfits in front of you, pleading with your partner to help you decide what to wear. You're feminine again.

I assume this entire time you were imagining it was you, with your gender identity, acting out that example. Now go back through the whole thing, but this time imagine someone with a different gender identity from you going through the motions. Now you are starting to understand how these concepts interrelate but don't interconnect.

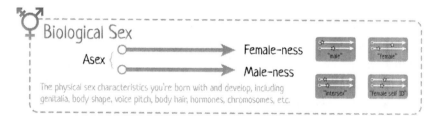

BIOLOGICAL SEX: THE EQUIPMENT UNDER THE HOOD

On the left we have "asex," which means without sex, and on the right we have "female-ness" and "male-ness" (both representing the degree to which you possess those characteristics). In the examples below, you see a new term, "intersex," which is a label for someone who has both male and female characteristics. You also see two "self ID" (self-identification) labels, which represent people who possess both male and female characteristics but identify with one of the binary sexes.

Biological sex refers to the objectively measurable organs, hormones, and chromosomes you possess. Let's consider biological sex in the ultra-reductive way society does: being female means having a vagina, ovaries, two X chromosomes, predominant estrogen, and the ability to grow a baby in your abdominal area; being male means having testes, a penis, an XY chromosome configuration, predominant testosterone, and the ability to put a baby in a female's abdominal area; and being intersex can be any combination of what I just described.

In reality, biological sex, like gender identity and expression, for most folks, is more nuanced than that. We will get to that in a later chapter, but for now I want to talk a bit more about intersex people.

For example, someone can be born with the appearance of being male (penis, scrotum, etc.), but have a functional female reproductive system inside. There are many examples of how intersex can present itself, and below you can see some statistics from the Intersex Society of North America illustrating the frequency of intersex births. (Check out the stat I bolded, but be prepared to be shocked.)

Not XX and Not XY	1 in 1,666 births
Klinefelter (XXY)	1 in 1,000 births
Androgen Insensitivity Syndrome	1 in 13,000 births
Partial Androgen Insensitivity Syndrome	1 in 130,000 births
Classical Congenital Adrenal Hyperplasia	1 in 13,000 births
Late Onset Adrenal Hyperplasia	1 in 66 individuals
Vaginal Agenesis	1 in 6,000 births
Ovotestes	1 in 6,000 births
Idiopathic (no discernible medical cause)	1 in 110,000 births
Iatrogenic (caused by medical treatment)	no estimate
5 Alpha Reductase Deficiency	no estimate
Mixed Gonadal Dysgenesis	no estimate
Complete Gonadal Dysgenesis	1 in 150,000 births
Hypospadias (in perineum or penile shaft)	1 in 2,000 births
Hypospadias (between corona and tip of penis)	1 in 770 births
Total number of people whose bodies differ from standard male or female	**1 in 100 births**
Total number of people receiving surgery to "normalize" genital appearance	1 or 2 in 1,000 births

In each grouping, circle all that apply to you and plot a point, depicting the aspects of gender toward which you experience attraction.

ATTRACTION: WHO YOU ARE ROMANTICALLY AND SEXUALLY INTO

On the left we have "nobody," meaning no feelings of attraction. On the right we have "men/males/masculinity" and "women/females/femininity." Examples below include "pansexual," which is attraction to all genders ("gender-blind"); "asexual," someone who experiences no (or little) sexual attraction (but might still experience romantic/other attraction); and "bisexual," a person attracted to people of both their gender and another gender.

Sexual orientation is all about who you are physically, spiritually, and emotionally attracted to (so really, you could plot three points on each of those continua, if you wanted to get really specific), and the labels tend to describe the relationships between your gender and the gender types you're attracted to.

If you are a man and you're attracted to women, you're straight. If you're a man who is attracted to men and another gender, you're bisexual. And if you're a man who is attracted to men, you're gay. This is the one most of us know the most about. We hear the most about it, it's salient in our lives, and we can best understand where we stand with it. It's pretty cut and dry, right? Maybe.

Interestingly enough, pioneering research conducted by Dr. Alfred Kinsey in the mid-twentieth century uncovered that most people aren't absolutely straight or gay/lesbian. Instead of just asking "Do you like dudes or chicks?" (very sciency, I know), he asked people to report their fantasies, dreams, thoughts, emotional investments in others, and frequency of sexual contact. Based on his findings, he broke sexuality down into a seven-point scale (see below), and reported that most people who identify as straight are actually somewhere between 1 and 3 on the scale, and most people who identify as lesbian/gay are between 3 and 5, meaning most of us are a little bi-.

0—Exclusively Heterosexual

1—Predominantly heterosexual, incidentally homosexual

2—Predominantly heterosexual, but more than incidentally homosexual

3—Equally heterosexual and homosexual

4—Predominantly homosexual, but more than incidentally heterosexual

5—Predominantly homosexual, incidentally heterosexual

6—Exclusively Homosexual

PUTTING IT ALL TOGETHER: INTERRELATION VS. INTERCONNECTION

Remember earlier when I said that thing and then said I would say it again? This is me saying that again: though the four things I presented above are certainly interrelated, they are not interconnected. What do I mean by that?

Gender identity, gender expression, biological sex, and sexual orientation are independent of one another (i.e., they are not connected).People's sexual orientation doesn't determine their gender expression. And their gender expression isn't determined by their gender identity. And their gender identity isn't determined by their biological sex. And also, every other mismatch of A isn't determined by B combination you can dream up from those inputs. Those things certainly affect one another (i.e., they are related to one another), but they do not determine one another.

If someone is born with male reproductive organs and genitalia, he is very likely to be raised as a boy, identify as a man, and express himself masculinely. We call this identity "cisgender" (when your biological sex aligns with how you identify), and it grants a lot of privilege (you already read about that, remember?). It's something most of us who have it don't appreciate nearly as much as we should.

CHAPTER 13

GENDER IDENTITY EXPLORED

THE PUBLIC HAVE AN INSATIABLE CURIOSITY TO KNOW EVERYTHING,
EXCEPT WHAT IS WORTH KNOWING.

—*Oscar Wilde*

The definition I provided for gender identity in the writing that accompanies the Genderbread Person, *who you think you are*, is a bit simplistic in scope, and I glossed over quite a bit in the explanation that followed. Let's talk a bit more about gender identity: what it means, where it comes from, and the roles it plays in our lives.

WHAT IS GENDER IDENTITY?

A society consists of a number of individuals who fill various social roles. These roles form our occupations (politician, teacher, doctor, farmer), establish family structures (mother, brother, daughter, uncle), and establish the terms of group and individual relationships (government and electorate, politician and voter, teacher and student).

Roles are established implicitly as a means of making sense and promoting order in a society. A number of societal needs must be met, and creating and fulfilling roles is one way we meet those needs. The roles that have existed the longest tend to have the clearest guidelines for the actors of the roles. They have been established and refined by hundreds (or thousands) of years of iteration and have been demonstrated to be valuable and necessary; in an ever-changing society, some needs have not changed much, and accordingly, the roles used to satisfy these needs have changed little as well.

There aren't many roles as old as gender roles, and therefore, there aren't many roles that are so clearly defined or immutable as gender roles.

Gender roles have always existed primarily to satisfy the need of a society to continue existing. Creating children and fostering their growth to self-sufficiency are the foundational needs that gender roles were created to meet. In modern societies, these needs are met more and more by a variety of specialized roles that exist outside of gender roles, yet we still perpetuate and reinforce gender roles in observance of tradition.

Unlike most roles, gender roles permeate and intersect with every other role individuals occupy, often resulting in compounded roles (e.g., consider the "female doctor" or "male teacher," where the person's gender role is bearing weight alongside—and sometimes more than—their occupational role). This obfuscates both the individual's gender and occupational roles, resulting in sometimes brackish combinations of the two that subvert social norms.

Gender identity is the way we, as individuals, make sense of how our bodies, personality characteristics, and predispositions align or don't align with established gender roles and norms.

WHAT'S THE DIFFERENCE BETWEEN GENDER IDENTITY AND GENDER ROLES?

Think about someone who is honest, has a strong sense of justice, and is responsible and articulate. Based on our understanding of norms, that person has characteristics that would lead them to fill the role of "judge." But let's imagine that person does not identify with the role of "judge" and instead identifies internally with the role of "entertainer" and decides to pursue a career in theatre.

Is that person wrong for not becoming a judge? Are they denying their biological or sociological imperative? Should they be corrected and assigned the role of judge?

The answer to all of those questions should be an emphatic "Nope!"

You could argue that this person's internal social identity is "entertainer" and that any other role they might fill, despite their alignment with what we would normally consider to be elements of that role, would result in dissonance between who they are and the role they fill.

This is very similar to how gender identity and gender roles relate to, and sometimes conflict with, one another.

Gender roles and norms are what we use to define and make sense of our gender identity (i.e., measure how much we align or don't align with what's been established to be man or woman to know if we are man, woman, or something else), but they are not the same thing. Think of gender roles and norms like the role of "judge" and the characteristics that comprise that role. Possessing certain characteristics may predispose someone to align with a particular gender identity, but it does not predetermine it.

Unlike in the example of the would-be judge, in instances where people's gendered characteristics don't align with the gender roles they fulfill (like with the would-be judge identifying as entertainer), they will not likely be met by a supportive and understanding society. This happens when a person's gender identity doesn't align with their gender expression or biological sex, and they choose to fulfill gender roles that align with their gender identity instead of the roles their external traits dictate they "should" fill.

For a lot of folks, this isn't a big issue. If someone is cisgender, where their gender identity aligns with their expression and sex, there is a good chance that the gender roles they will be pushed to fulfill will at least partially align with their identity.

However, at the same time, few people *completely* align with all aspects of a particular gender role, whether they are cis or trans*, meaning that the pressure for anyone to conform fully to gender roles will generally lead to at least a small amount of identity dissonance.

SO, WE BASE OUR GENDER IDENTITY ON GENDER ROLES, BUT GENDER ROLES INHERENTLY CONFLICT WITH OUR GENDER IDENTITY?

Yep. And it's a real bummer. There's an explanation for why this happens, but to understand it, you may have to take a leap: gender is a social construction based on a misattribution of a biological imperative.

Remember how I told you earlier that gender roles are one of the earliest, and they originally existed to support the population growth of a society? At our most basic, instinctual levels, we have an urge to reproduce. But after establishing that primal urge for reproduction, our brains continued to develop, and we now have capacities for reasoning and feel the need to have greater meaning in our lives (greater than just making miniature versions of us). Gender roles are one of the ways we have made sense of this urge to reproduce and reconciled it with our higher needs and yearning for meaning.

The conflict comes into play when we take something that is a pure biological imperative (reproduction) and try to make sense of it in a social manner (gender).

The capacity for sexual reproduction is objectively classifiable. A scientist can biologically measure a person from any area on the planet's ability to reproduce and pair that person up with another person who is a reproductive match from any other area on the planet.

Gender is not objectively classifiable. You cannot objectively measure or compare a person's gender with that of another person across cultural borders. Gender is a relative, social construction that varies extremely widely among humans.

We have done a great job of connecting sexual reproduction (and the biological components necessary to do so) with a social role and personality predisposition. And in doing so we have created a couple roles (man and woman) that we expect an infinite number of identities (a unique interpretation of self for each person on Earth) to fit into.

SO WHAT IS GENDER IDENTITY?

Now that we've done a lot of unpacking and rearranging of understanding, let's answer this question again. What is gender identity?

You've likely realized by now that there really is no simple answer to this question. Gender identity is how you internally define yourself in terms of what you understand gender to be, but that's really just the surface-level answer.

Let's go a bit deeper

Gender identity is our internal response to a social construction that attempts to make a connection between a person's biological makeup and their eventual role in society. It is a social analog to a biological classification that conflates a person's reproductive capacity with their personality and predispositions, and limits us to a few constricting (and problematic) social roles to align with the few biological roles inherent in our anatomy.

Even deeper

Gender identity is a reductive version of categorizing personality. It's a way for us fit everyone on earth into a few broad categories ("man," "woman," "other"), in hopes that this will add some order to the chaos that is interpersonal life. We take all the personality traits available to people, divide them into two groups, assign everyone (with their infinitely different personalities) to one of those personality group options (based on something unrelated to personality), and—*Voila!*—now we know how to treat everyone!

HOWDY Just want to check in and make sure everything is going okay. This chapter got pretty intense at the end, and we are only about halfway down this rabbit hole. Allow me to reiterate that it's okay to reread (no shame!), take a break (strongly encouraged!), or ask for clarification (phone a friend!). Also did you know that "Howdy" comes from "How do you do?" I mean, *talk about reductive.*

CHAPTER 14

GENDER EXPRESSION EXPLORED

IF I'M NOT WITH A BUTCH EVERYONE JUST ASSUMES I'M STRAIGHT.
IT'S LIKE I'M PASSING TOO, AGAINST MY WILL. I'M SICK OF THE WORLD
THINKING I'M STRAIGHT. I'VE WORKED HARD TO BE DISCRIMINATED
AGAINST AS A LESBIAN.

—*Leslie Feinberg*

Gender expression, *how you demonstrate who you are*, is a relatively simple concept to understand—at least compared to gender identity. Though simpler than gender identity, gender expression is the aspect of gender that has the most influence on your interactions with others.

Gender expression is what most determines the adversity you will face as a result of your gender. It is also what most determines the privilege you will experience as a result of your gender. Gender expression is often confused with sexuality, which is the reason I ended up sitting here writing this and you ended up sitting wherever you are reading it. Sounds like we have a lot to talk about.

WHAT IS GENDER EXPRESSION?

Gender expression is a way of labeling how much someone does or does not present in ways that are traditionally gendered. We usually describe someone's expression as masculine or feminine, and when neither is particularly salient, we have androgyny (three concepts that are brought to us courtesy of gender norms).

Gender expression is generally discussed in terms of gender norms. This is important to remember because while gender norms enable us to use terms like "feminine" or "masculine" and have a universal (within the scope of a particular culture) idea of what we are talking about, they are also drastically different from culture to culture.

For example, if we didn't define wearing tights as "feminine" then wearing tights would just be wearing tights. Further, until a couple hundred years ago many western cultures would have viewed tights as "masculine," or at least "androgynous." Even further, tights—or more accurately, "meggings" (man + leggings)—might be becoming trendy again for men to wear, particularly in the United Kingdom. My, what a topsy-turvy world we live in.

But gender expression goes far beyond clothing.

Gender expression encompasses all the ways you present yourself that are governed by gender norms, which, as you likely now realize, is just about everything. Clothing, mannerisms, gait, pitch of voice, language choices, pronunciation of language, posture, grooming, social interactions, and much, much more all go into what we would merge together in our minds to be an individual's gender expression.

WHAT DETERMINES YOUR GENDER EXPRESSION?

Gender expression can be a way of demonstrating your gender identity, but it can also be an intentional way of rejecting your gender identity. It can align with the gender norms attached to your biological sex, or not. It can be driven by your want to conform, your want to rebel, sexual or relational desires, or something else altogether. It can make perfect sense to you as you look in a mirror and reflect on who you are or may make no sense at all and leave you confused and wondering what drives you to wear pants so tight you regularly rip them while dancing—or maybe that's just me?

Or, the shorter version: the determining factors in an individual's gender expression are as diverse as the ways individuals express gender.

If you are socialized in a way that allows for more flexibility in your gender expression, there is a good chance you will express gender more flexibly. If, however, you were socialized with strict, rigid norms pertaining to gender expression, you are likely to follow those norms and express gender in a normalized way.

But neither of those are guarantees. Plenty of folks brought up in households where it would have been just as OK for boys to wear dresses and girls to wear ties still express gender in traditional ways. And plenty of folks brought up in households where it might be dangerous for a boy to wear a dress or a girl to wear a tie still express gender in nontraditional ways.

GENDER EXPRESSION IS FLUID AND HARD TO CATEGORIZE

Gender expression, unlike gender identity, is not something you establish at an early age and stick with your entire life. It's something that is always changing, whether you intend for it to or not.

What society considers "feminine" and "masculine" changes

Even if you try to dress, behave, interact, and present yourself the same way your entire life, the implications of those actions changes. Style, demeanor, and all the other things that make up gender expression change on a regular basis, sometimes as often as from season to season.

What you try to express may be interpreted otherwise

As much as your intention in expressing gender matters, how that expression is received and interpreted matters more, at least if we are talking in terms of affecting your interactions with others. Individuals will interpret gender expressions using a lens unique to them—based on their experiences, their predispositions, and a number of other variables.

Labels for gender expression like "femme" and "butch" have limited effectiveness

While terms describing gender expressions certainly exist, their ability to convey universally understood meaning isn't nearly as effective as terms for gender identities. Part of this is because many of these terms come from relatively small subcultures, but in general, these terms are troublesome because of how broad the range of gender expression is, even within gender expression labels like "femme" or "butch."

WHAT ARE THE EFFECTS OF GENDER EXPRESSION?

Gender expression is, in society's eye, inexorably linked to sexuality, gender identity, and biological sex. Most folks think it's not just linked to but predetermined by those things. This is not a healthy misconception, and it results in a lot of "not healthy" (euphemism) outcomes. Let's start small and build up.

Gender expression can cause others to confuse your identity

This is what I was referring to earlier when I said gender expression confusions have led us here. This is what led to the creation of *It's Pronounced Metrosexual* and has put me in hundreds of situations where I've found myself explaining to people that I'm not gay. It has nothing to do with my sexuality but everything to do with my gender expression.

Due to the connection people draw between gender and sexuality, and the feminine ways I tend to express gender (through language, demeanor, dress, and grooming), I am always experiencing this gender confusion side effect. Gender expression also leads folks to incorrectly assume someone's gender identity (I'm sure you've heard someone ask, or asked yourself, "Is that a dude or a chick?").

This little misunderstanding has affected my life in a more drastic way than is likely typical (you know, determining my career), but there are plenty more folks than me who experience friction on a daily basis because of this. And friction isn't fun when you're just trying to be *you*.

The pressure to express gender in a particular way can lead to anxiety and depression

We feel a lot of pressure to be cisgender. If you are, you can live where you want, eat where you want, and pee where you want—all good things. For folks who aren't cisgender, attempting to "pass" as cis by way of gender expression is one way to give into this pressure.

Similarly, we feel a lot of pressure to be straight. Due to the connections we draw between gender and sexuality, people who are queer may also give into the pressures of heteronormativity and do their best to express "straight" (e.g., men expressing masculinely, women expressing femininely).

Giving into pressure to express in a way other than how you're comfortable leads to identity dissonance—a gap between your inner self and the self you are presenting to the world—that can lead to anxiety and depression.

Resisting the pressure to express gender in a particular way and expressing it how you are comfortable can also lead to dissonance between you and those around you who are pushing you to conform (and giving into those pressures themselves). This too can increase your likelihood of experiencing anxiety and depression.

Dang. But don't worry. It only gets worse.

Your gender expression can put you at risk for serious bodily harm

I'm not going to spend much time explaining this unfortunate outcome of gender expression, so just take my word for it or do some Internet searching later.

If it doesn't fit into some people's boxes of acceptable options, the way you express your gender can provoke them to threaten, attack, and in some particularly horrifying cases, kill you. This seems to most commonly happen in bathrooms, locker rooms, and other gender-defined spaces.

BUT IT'S NOT ALL BAD: GENDER EXPRESSION IS ALSO A LOT OF FUN

Wow. This chapter got heavy fast. It's important not to gloss over the sad stuff, but I also think it's important we realize that while it's not all sunshine and rainbows, it's also not all storm clouds and killer leprechauns waiting at the ends of those rainbows.

One of my favorite aspects of gender expression is the ability to have fun with it, experiment with different ways of expressing gender to see how they feel. It's like trying on clothes, but instead of clothes you get to try on different types of language, mannerisms, demeanors, and—well, yes—clothes.

DRILL: "Try on" another gender expression for a bit. Wear clothing that aligns with a gender expression you don't typically express, behave in ways you consider more masculine or feminine than normal (do both!), the whole package. Do this in a safe space, where you are around people who make you feel comfortable, and remember that "a gender expression you don't typically express" doesn't mean "act like a 'woman' if you're a man, or a 'man' if you're a woman" (e.g., it would make me far more uncomfortable to express ultramasculine than super feminine, even though I'm a man). We're past all that binary stuff by now, right? Phew.

A lot of the more extreme gender expressions you see are just this: a show of sorts, or at the least a conscious presentation. Drag is the most recognizable example of this, but you see more subtle examples all the time. A formal dinner party tends to bring out the extremes in feminine (dresses, makeup, fancy woman hair) and masculine (suits, ties, fancy man hair). People often get hilariously masculine while playing sports (I grunt, I'm not ashamed to admit it) and hilariously feminine while watching *The Lion King* (I cry every time).

See, gender expression can be fun. And it will be all fun when we're finally in a place as a society where we realize gender identity, biological sex, and sexual orientation interrelate with gender expression, but they do not determine it. And where people feel comfortable, and above all safe, expressing gender however they please.

The Most Manly 'Do in the Class Award goes to...

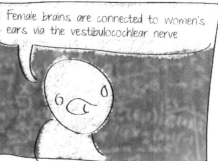

CHAPTER 15

BIOLOGICAL SEX EXPLORED

IN BIOLOGY, NOTHING IS CLEAR, EVERYTHING IS TOO COMPLICATED, EVERYTHING IS A MESS, AND JUST WHEN YOU THINK YOU UNDERSTAND SOMETHING, YOU PEEL OFF A LAYER AND FIND DEEPER COMPLICATIONS BENEATH. NATURE IS ANYTHING BUT SIMPLE.

—Richard Preston

People tend to easily come to the understanding that gender identity and gender expression are more varied than we learned as kids, but biological sex is generally a hang-up. "How can someone be more male or more female than someone else?" There are a few ways to look at this, but let's start with the basics.

WHAT IS BIOLOGICAL SEX?

Biological sex is the phrase we use to categorize the physical anatomy someone has, based on how it aligns with what we understand to be "intersex," "female," or "male." The easiest way to examine these labels is with example characteristics.

Characteristics of male biological sex include testes; penis; 46,XY karyotype; more testosterone than estrogen; thick body hair; facial hair; wide shoulders; and a deep-pitched voice.

Characteristics of female biological sex include ovaries; vagina; uterus; 46,XX karyotype; more estrogen than testosterone; breasts; fine body hair; fine (or no) facial hair; wide hips; and a high-pitched voice.

Characteristics of intersex biological sex include combinations of male and female characteristics above, in addition to unique karyotypes like 46,XY DSD; 46,XX DSD; 46,XY CGD; and 47,XXY.

If someone has all the characteristics of male biological sex, we label them as "male." If someone has all the characteristics of female biological sex, we label them as "female." And if someone has characteristics associated with both sexes, we will either label them as "intersex" or alter their anatomy and label them "female" or "male" (whichever is closer).

THE EFFECT OF BIOLOGICAL SEX

Due to the incomplete way we understand gender, the biological sex someone is assigned at birth is also seen as a gender identity assignment. If you're male at birth, you're a boy, and we're going to raise you to be a man. If you're female at birth, you're a girl, and we're going to raise you to be a woman. And if you're intersex at birth, we have to figure it out (more on this later).

In most cases, this assignment means a child is beginning to be socialized into one of the binary genders from birth on. If the child happens to have a gender identity that aligns with the gender norms they are being socialized to adhere to, there isn't much of an issue. Although there is a lot to be said about gender-neutral parenting and the general benefits of this practice (that help cis and trans* youth alike in their development), I'll leave that for a book about gender-neutral parenting.

The problem is when the one in 100 kids who aren't cisgender are being socialized as though they are, pushed to adopt norms that don't align with their identities, creating a confusing worldview at a young age—and all in response to a biological sex assignment at birth.

SEX ASSIGNMENT FOR INTERSEX BABIES

As I mentioned a few times, a sex (usually male or female) is assigned to a baby even if that baby is born intersex. How does that work? It depends on how ambiguous the baby's sex is at birth.

Slightly ambiguous genitalia

If a baby is born with genitalia that are ambiguous enough for a doctor to notice, the doctors will tentatively make a sex assignment and then perform a few simple tests before making it official. A typical example of ambiguous genitalia present at birth would be an enlarged clitoris in an otherwise "female" body. The tests the doctors will conduct range from chromosome tests, hormone levels, or ultrasounds to check for sex organs. Once the results of these tests come back, assuming they reflect what the doctors originally suspected, they will confirm the sex assignment.

Completely ambiguous genitalia

If a baby is born with genitalia that are too ambiguous for a doctor to make a sex assignment, the process is a bit more drawn out. The doctors will have to guess and check hypotheses using elaborate tests, sometimes relying on endocrinologists' suggestions, and use surgical interventions to eventually adjust the genitals of the baby to align with whatever sex they decide is best for the child.

Criteria used in sex assignment for intersex babies

The criteria for making sex assignments has changed a bit in the last sixty years, and I don't want to get lost in the nitty-gritty details in this book (rigid algorithms are used to make sex decisions based on type of karyotypes and other characteristics), so let me paint you a general picture of how this works, and you can research it and learn more later if you'd like.

In the cases above, where a baby is born with ambiguous genitalia, doctors are put in a position where they attempt to assign the child a sex that will lead to the least gender and social conflict later in life. It's generally accepted in the medical community that sex and gender aren't the same thing (gender is viewed as "nurture" while sex is "nature"), which is fantastic, but the problem lies with how this information is used.

Instead of saying, "We don't know what this kid's gender will end up being, so let's hold off on assigning a sex," they say, "We don't know what this kid's gender will end up being, so let's assign them a sex and tell their parents to socialize them into the gender that corresponds with the sex we assigned them. Yeah, that'll work out just fine."

So close. They have the right idea of the problem, but a patently wrong idea of the solution.

HOW CAN SOMEONE BE DIFFERENT DEGREES OF A PARTICULAR SEX?

The way I have sex depicted in the Genderbread Person model, there are varying degrees of "male-ness" or "female-ness" an individual can possess. "What do you mean by that?" I get asked by confused people. "That doesn't make sense, does it?" I hear frustrated people wonder. "Tell me your ATM pin code!" the confused, frustrated people demand. I get robbed.

Biological sex is a bit of a misnomer because it tears the term out of the sociological (or psychological) world where gender typically lives. A lot of folks protest my use of the word "biological" in "biological sex," and would prefer I just said "sex."

I use it that way on the Genderbread Person graphic, and in turn in my writing explaining the graphic, because I am trying to debunk the idea of gender = sex, and I find that "biological sex" is a better starting point than "sex" (ambiguous, commonly used in exchange for "gender") or "physical sex" (which gets giggles, 'cuz I don't know any other way to do it).

That said, sex is as much a social construct as it is a biological one. Sure, you are born with what we call "sex characteristics" (like all the ones mentioned in the lists above). That part's biological. But the way we make meaning of those characteristics is all sociology, baby.

Beyond the most basic understanding of sex, the reproductive understanding, our entire understanding of sex (and its impact on our lives) is formed by how we are socialized. Almost all of the sex characteristics I listed above (from body shape to pitch of voice) are determined by sex steroid (hormone) levels during adolescence.

The more your body is pumping out and receiving androgens (like testosterone), the more "male-ness" you'll develop; and the more estrogens your body makes and utilizes, the more "female-ness" you'll develop. And while development of hormones is strongly linked to your "sex," there is a huge amount of variation in levels (much more than the three categories of variation "sex" affords).

Examples of male-ness in me: wide shoulders (not bragging), testes, beard, hard jaw and brow lines, penis (still not bragging).

Examples of female-ness in me: lack of protruding Adam's apple, fine body hair, wide [child-bearing] hips (bragging), relatively high-pitched voice.

Starting to think the term "male" might not apply that well? Me too. But it'd be misleading to label me "intersex."

Uh oh. Mr. Spock, what do you make of this?

"Quite simply, Captain, I examined the problem from all angles, and it was plainly hopeless. Logic informed me that under the circumstances, the only logical action would have to be one of desperation. Logical decision, logically arrived at."

Desperation it is.

CHAPTER 16

ATTRACTION & GENDER

THAT'S ALWAYS SEEMED SO RIDICULOUS TO ME, THAT PEOPLE WANT TO BE AROUND SOMEONE BECAUSE THEY'RE PRETTY. IT'S LIKE PICKING YOUR BREAKFAST CEREALS BASED ON COLOR INSTEAD OF TASTE.

—*John Green*

We understand that sexual orientation and gender are separate but interrelated concepts. This is relatively easily understood within the contexts of cisgender identities. But how does sexual orientation "work" for people who are genderqueer?

Before we address attraction as it plays out with genderqueer folks, I want to focus on attraction as a general idea, and then we can move into the more complex stuff.

Also, it's worth noting that "sexual orientation" itself is a loaded—and in some ways limiting—term. I'm using it here to employ at least one term most people are familiar with and to describe a combination of physical, emotional/romantic, and spiritual attraction. Sexuality is a complicated subject that deserves a book entirely to itself, but as the focus of this book is gender, I will only be scratching the surface of sexuality as it relates to gender.

BEGINNING TO UNDERSTAND ATTRACTION

Attraction is a powerful—and can feel like an inexplicable—force for those who feel it. The draw to a specific grouping of characteristics, your "type," or to moods and feelings that are elicited by certain people is a mysterious force, but it's not inexplicable. It's quite explicable. Let's explicate it. (Bet you didn't know that was a word. Even I was surprised when a red squiggly didn't pop up underneath it.)

DRILL: Write down examples of the types of people or characteristics you are attracted to romantically, physically/sexually, and emotionally/spiritually. Categorize these things into traditional gendered categories (feminine/masculine, man/woman, male/female) as you come up with them, and then share and discuss your list with a friend who did the same thing. If you've never explored or considered this, really spend some time (thirty to forty-five minutes, to start) on it before you continue reading.

ATTRACTION IS IN YOUR HEAD, LIKE AN IMAGINARY FRIEND

For a moment, stop thinking in terms of cisgender versus genderqueer and instead think just think about attraction. Attraction is something that comes from within. There are a lot of theories on what drives attraction—or where it comes from.

I buy into the theory that attraction is the result of your subconscious interpretation of hormonal influences on your brain chemistry, and your ability to make sense of attraction is a result of your socialization and self-awareness. That is, attraction is largely out of your control, but how you make sense of it and act upon it is up to you.

This understanding of attraction applies equally to both cisgender and genderqueer folks.

It's about who you're attracted to, not you

Still just thinking about attraction in general (rather than cisgender attraction versus genderqueer attraction), which do you think plays a larger role in the attraction dance: the other person's identity(ies), or yours?

A lot of cisgender straight people would say that if they became the opposite gender (through magic, I guess—perhaps a spell woven by Åndrøgyne, a Gender Mage of the Circle of... too far?), they would still be straight. You've probably heard a straight cis- guy say something like "If I was a girl, I would totally be into Brad Pitt."

Guess what, dude: you're into Brad Pitt.

Sexual orientation and gender aren't dependent on one another like that. If you suddenly became a different gender, you would still be attracted to the same type of people, or you would no longer be you.

Now this is smudgy, because one could argue that if you became a different gender, you would likely have a different mix of hormones floating around inside your hat rack, which might have influenced your attraction, but we're not going to go there. Remember, there was magic involved.

What's important is that attraction—truly, absolutely distilled and rinsed—is about the other, not about the you (or, for all the grammar nerds, it's about the object, not the subject). Though that might be hard to imagine ("I've just always imagined my penis going into a vagina," a guy told me once, to my mirth), it is the case. Or it's at least most of the case.

Understanding identity is like utilizing the light side of the force: there are no absolutes (except for the one absolute absolving that there are none, of course).

UPDATING OUR TERMINOLOGY

In order to make this as clear as we can, we need to be speaking the same language. Conventional terms to describe sexual orientation (hetero-, homo-, and bisexual) don't work well outside of the cisgender world, because they are dependent on the gender relationship between the attracted and the attractee (or the subject and the object of, in some cases, doin' it). Many have argued that I shouldn't use those terms at all in my gender writings because they aren't inclusive of genderqueer folks. While that's true, the conventional (and non-genderqueer-inclusive) terms are more accessible to people who are new to these concepts, which is why I kept them in place.

New terms for expressing sexual orientation

Androsexual/Androphilic: attracted to males, men, and/or masculinity

Gynesexual/Gynephilic: attracted to females, women, and/or femininity

Skoliosexual: attracted to genderqueer and transsexual people and expressions (people who aren't identified as cisgender)

Pansexual: attracted to all types of people, regardless of biological sex, gender identity, or expression

Asexual/Nonsexual: no sexual attraction, but often romantic or spiritual attractions exist

NOTE: for all of these terms, attraction can be further broken down into romantic, sexual/physical, and emotional/spiritual attraction (e.g., a person may be romantically androphilic but sexually gynephilic).

Limitations of these terms, and in general

The terms presented above are far better than the conventional terms for describing sexual orientation, but they are certainly not perfect. You have to remember: identities are far too numerous for any list, graph, or book chapter to describe them all. Some would argue that the list above, for example, isn't super inclusive of third-gender (or fourth-, or some-) folks, or two-spirit folks, but it's another step toward understanding an incredibly complex concept. When in doubt, rely on the Platinum Rule.

SO, HOW DOES GENDERQUEER SEXUAL ORIENTATION WORK?

Just from reading the terms above, you should start to have a basic understanding of how attraction works for our genderqueer friends. If you're particularly quick, you'll realize it's not really different from how it works for our cisgender friends. Not quite there yet? It'll be my pleasure to explain.

In short, genderqueer sexual orientation works just like cisgender sexual orientation works. People are attracted to certain kinds of people; attracted to certain expressions of masculinity and femininity; attracted to certain physical manifestations of sex and gender (breasts and/or hair and/or penises and/or etc.); and attracted to a certain gender or certain self-identities as they pertain to relationship and societal roles.

If a genderqueer person is attracted to women, you would say that person is gynesexual. If a cisgender person (man or woman) is attracted to women, you would also say that person is gynesexual. If a genderqueer person is attracted to genderqueer people, you would say that person is skoliosexual. If a cisgender person (man or woman) is attracted to genderqueer people, you would say that person is skoliosexual (see how much more inclusive these terms are?).

So let me say it again: genderqueer sexual orientation works just like cisgender sexual orientation works. In fact, those "new terms for expressing sexual orientation" work just as well for cisgender people as they do for genderqueer people.

Some (I) would argue we should do a better job adopting them into our vocabularies, but some (I) also understand that just beginning to understand the complexity of gender is already a lot to ask.

IT CAN'T BE THAT SIMPLE

No, of course not. Nothing in identity is actually simple. But it can be simplified to be this simple, and it just was. The sooner we stop thinking of genderqueer people as "the other" and stop finding more ways to differentiate between cisgender and genderqueer, the sooner we'll begin to understand one another, accept one another, and legislate fairly for one as well as the other.

Hopefully, at least that last one.

The oft-misunderstood Transsaurus Rex

CHAPTER 17

AN ASSORTMENT OF GENDER IDENTITIES

IF EVERY EVENT WHICH OCCURRED COULD BE GIVEN A NAME, THERE WOULD BE NO NEED FOR STORIES.

—*John Berger*

Defining and labeling specific gender identities creates a system of understanding that's as reliable as the hyperdrive on the Millennium Falcon. That is, relying too heavily on them often leads to more bad than good, but when they work they can make the Kessel Run in less than 12 parsecs.

The benefit of labeling identities, as I've said before and will continue to say forever, is that they create solidarity, a shared experience, and a support system for a community. The downside is that people rarely embody every trait of any particular identity label.

In the spirit of that duality, I am presenting in this chapter an alphabetically-arranged guide to the many gender identity labels I know of*, with the best explanations and backgrounds for each that I can muster, but also with anonymous accounts of individuals (sent to me via email) who self-identify with those labels explaining what they mean to them.

The ones I left out were either done so intentionally (I don't know enough about the identity to feel comfortable writing about it, or I couldn't find a person who had that identity to write their part) or by accident (less likely). In both cases, I apologize for anyone who feels underrepresented or marginalized.

NOTE: this is a brave new world, and the list of "gender identity labels I know of" is perpetually incomplete due to the constant advent of new identities. Don't think that because you hear of something you don't see here that it's any less real or deserves any less respect than the identities in this chapter.

AGENDER (SOMETIMES GENDER NEUTROIS, GENDER NEUTRAL, OR GENDERLESS)

Agender people have no connection to the traditional system of gender, no personal alignment with the concepts of either "man" or "woman," and see themselves as existing without gender. They often don't have any connection to the ideas of masculinity or femininity and may attempt to present gender (or alter their secondary sex characteristics) in ways that don't embody aspects of either.

Agender is a relatively new term to describe a particular type of gender nonconformity. Estimates of "gender nonconforming" folks within the trans* community hover around 10 percent, and there are no good numbers on what percentage of these folks may identify as agender (or similarly).

"I was born female, but it never clicked. If it were up to me, I wouldn't have nipples. My ideal physical body would be without genitalia or breasts, and I prefer when people refer to me as 'they.' I came out two times in my life (once as a lesbian, then as a transman) before realizing that my issue wasn't with attraction or figuring out what gender I was but was with gender itself. I don't feel it the way other people seem to."

BIGENDER

Bigender (not to be confused with genderfluid) people fully identify with two separate genders, often "man" and "woman," or any two gender identities. For some bigender people, this means switching between the two gender identities throughout the day, week, or year; for others, their embodied gender is a bit more gray, hovering between the two at any given time, but they still fully identify with both.

For bigender people whose biological sex and assigned gender align with one of their gender identities (essentially making them "half" cisgender), it can be difficult not to defer to that gender identity at all times, thereby creating dissonance with their other identity. This issue can be similarly troublesome during a bigender person's coming out process, as the people in their life may continue to only see them as a cisgender person and may not recognize the other gender identity they embody within.

"A lot of people think of gender as a continuum, and that's fine, but I see it more like apples and oranges. Some people are apples, some people are oranges, some people are grapes, etc. For me, I just happen to be an apple and a grape—like a fruit salad. At times you'll taste 100 percent apple. Others it's 100 percent grape. Others it's a bite with both, so you taste them both at the same time. But I'm not a grapple. I'm a grape, and I'm an apple. I fully align with "man" just as much as I fully align with "woman."

GENDERFLUID

Genderfluid (not to be confused with bigender) people experience varying gender identities at different times. For some genderfluid people, this means shifting slowly back and forth along a spectrum from one gender to another through a day, month, or year; the identities of other genderfluid people shift more based on particular situations they may find themselves in (e.g., when around certain people or other genders, or engaged in activities that they might consider to be more suitable for a particular gender).

The core trait of someone who is genderfluid is the idea that their gender is dynamic. The actual genders different genderfluid people identify with can be any of the gender identities mentioned in this chapter, and the number of options someone flows between as well as how that flow happens is different for different genderfluid people.

"When I was younger, my parents thought I suffered from chronic depression because I would consistently go through phases where I was

despondent and just turned off from the world. As I grew up, I realized this was just my gender shifting from woman to man, and my body not knowing how to make sense of it. I would feel completely outside of myself, because I was a girl and didn't feel like a girl for a few months, but then it would all come back to normal for a while. I've since realized what was happening and can support the boy part of me when it comes out better and not feel like an alien in my own body every couple of months."

GENDERQUEER (SOMETIMES TRANS*, OR GENDERBENDER)

Genderqueer (and sometimes trans* or genderbender) is often used as an umbrella term for anyone who doesn't identify within the gender binary, meaning that genderqueer isn't an identity itself but rather a grouping of identities (e.g., someone who is bigender is also genderqueer). Some people who are genderqueer are also transgender.

But some folks identify simply as genderqueer, embracing the ambiguity of the term and demonstrating that the only certainty in their gender identity is that it's not 100 percent man or 100 percent woman. People who identify their gender as genderqueer often express gender in ways that combine clashing gender norms regarding masculinity and femininity and may see gender and sex as separate aspects of identity, stating they are a "male woman" or a "female man," and they often transcend the gender binary completely.

"I see saying I'm genderqueer the same way someone might say they are agnostic: I believe that gender exists, and I have it, but it's beyond me to say that I can comfortably define what it is. If you think you know what gender is, and are sure about yours, I think you're making a leap of faith."

MAN (ALSO TRANSMAN, TRANS MAN, OR FTM MAN)

A person who identifies as a man aligns fully—or at least mostly—with the roles and norms ascribed to people born male in a society. This person has no personal friction with the options presented by the traditional gender binary.

A lot of people who identify as men have never questioned that identity and are simply expressing and embodying the traits they were taught to be appropriate for men at childhood.

A lot of men who were born male and have explored gender do not fully align with all aspects of "man-ness" but still identify as man because it mostly represents them, or because they don't want to trivialize the struggles of trans* people.

For transmen, trans men, or FtM (Female-to-Male) men, while they were not born male, they have likely always identified as men, or realized upon exploring what gender meant to them that they were men.

"It makes sense to me that I'm a man. I like manly things, and I'm comfortable around other men. I'm not super athletic and have a job as a teacher, which I guess to some people might make me 'less of a man,' but I see being a man more as being comfortable in the gender I've always had and never feeling any pressure from inside that something wasn't right."

WOMAN (ALSO TRANSWOMAN, TRANS WOMAN, OR MTF WOMAN)

A person who identifies as a woman aligns fully—or, at least, mostly—with the roles and norms ascribed to people born female in a society. This person has no personal friction with the options presented by the traditional gender binary.

A lot of people who identify as women have never questioned that identity and are simply expressing and embodying the traits they were taught to be appropriate for women at childhood.

A lot of women who were born female and have explored gender do not fully align with all aspects of "woman-ness" but still identify as woman because it mostly represents them, or because they don't want to trivialize the struggles of trans* people.

For transwomen, trans women, or MtF (Male-to-Female) women, while they were not born female, they have likely always identified as women, or realized upon exploring what gender meant to them that they were women.

"As a kid, seeing the girls on TV playing with Barbies, I was always

like, 'Yes, that is so me. That's my friends. That's my life.' I never needed another option. I was a pink girl. I was a fashion girl. I want a career, but I also want to be a mom—yes, a 'mom,' not a 'parent.' There's a difference."

TRANSGENDER

Transgender is generally understood to be an umbrella term for anyone whose gender identity doesn't match the sex they were assigned at birth (essentially the opposite of cisgender). Many folks' identities could be best understood as "transgender and..." (e.g., transgender and third-gender), in that transgender is an all-encompassing term that binds many of the other gender identities together.

The umbrella term "transgender" is great because it can be used in a constructive way to lump together all of the diverse gender identities and create a sense of group cohesion. This is helpful for civil rights purposes (transgender people fighting for "transgender rights" as a group is much more effective than bigender people fighting for "bigender rights" while genderfluid people fight for "genderfluid rights" and so on).

The identity label "transgender" is troublesome because it's often mischaracterized as describing "a woman trapped in a man's body" (and vice versa), which is not only a damaging way to view gender and sex but also an incredibly generalizing way to convey a term that is used to describe people of incredibly diverse gender individual identities and experiences.

As an identity label, folks who solely identify as transgender have many different interpretations of what this means. For some, it's interchangeable with the identity label "non-binary" (meaning a person who neither identifies as man nor woman), for others it has elements of genderfluid or genderqueer (another label that is often interchangeable with transgender, when used as an identity). Due to this wide range, I would rather not include a specific example of someone who uses the identity label "transgender," because it will likely be more misleading (in its specificity) than helpful (in its ability to be generalized).

Instead, I want to end with a passage from someone who has an identity label so specific you will not likely see it in any list, but one that embodies how personal and individual gender really is:

"Some view gender as if there is no middle-ground – the only options are "male" or "female." Personally, I identify as a genderqueer trans*boi and due to hormones and surgery, I pass as a cisman even in trans*spaces. I often hear the words "femme," "Why bother transitioning if you're going to do drag?" and "Is that dude rocking a beard and glitter nail polish?" used in reference to me. A lot of the time I identify as "mostly male", which is why I chose to undergo a medical transition, but I'm never "completely male" (or "completely female" either!); usually my gender falls somewhere in the middle, a mixing-pot of male and female and everything else in between, and am happiest when my presentation causes people to second-guess themselves."

CHAPTER 18

HOW TO DIAGNOSE SOMEONE AS TRANSGENDER

HE EXPLAINED TO ME WITH GREAT INSISTENCE THAT EVERY QUESTION POSSESSED A POWER THAT DID NOT LIE IN THE ANSWER.

—*Elie Wiesel*

If you immediately flipped to this chapter because after opening the book and looking at the table of contents, you saw this and were excited because this was one of the things you were hoping to learn from this book—tricked you!

If you immediately flipped to this chapter because after opening the book and looking at the table of contents, you were mortified—worry not!

And if you are reading this chapter because you just finished reading the chapter before it…well, ignore those first two paragraphs. Start with the next one.

This one.

Actually, start with this one: you can't "diagnose" "someone" "as transgender." That's a weird way to quote that, but I want to break that troublesome statement down into those three separate, troublesome parts. Before I do that, let me talk about this idea of diagnosing someone as transgender in general.

I initially wanted to have this chapter in the book, with this title, and simply have the entire contents of the chapter be "You can't."

Then I thought it'd be funnier to have it be "you can't you can't you can't" repeated over and over and over like I was Jack in *The Shining*.

These super funny "jokes" I came up with are the result of the myriad times I've been asked this question, both in person after giving talks or performing and also via e-mail or comments on the web. Initially, I would respond with a long, drawn-out explanation (see the rest of this chapter) unpacking the issues with this question, but over time I simplified, breaking it down more and more until my response eventually became "You can't." Just those two words. Then I would move on to the next question.

I have gone with this response in person, and I recommend it to anyone and everyone because I found that while my comprehensive explanations conveyed a lot of the rationale behind "You can't," they also allowed other people to have wiggle room in their rationales for asking the question to begin with. That is, every point I'll address in this chapter brings with it counterpoints that folks may mull in their mind or argue out loud. The conversation then becomes a debate and people get defensive, and nobody learns when they're defensive. That's why there is so much beauty in "You can't."

"You can't" isn't an answer to the question so much as it is pointing at some fact of nature. It's like if you were to ask someone how much it hurt when they got punched in the head, and as a response they punched you in the head. Now you know. "You can't" is that punch in the head (but without all the fun violence), because it dismisses any other possibilities, rhetoric, or creative debate that might crop up. Like how someone might think, "I wonder if it would hurt more if I wasn't expecting to be punched in the hea—." No need to wonder. They *know*.

Another great thing about "You can't" is it's also a great response to use when someone asks me "How can you tell when someone is gay?" One answer, perfect for two questions I get asked all the time. So helpful.

But the best thing about "You can't" is it ends the discussion. We can move on. And when someone asks "Why not?" I punch them in the head. Not because I'm violent, but because I am not sure if they were going to ask what getting punched in the head feels like eventually, and I'm a giver.

Now let's talk about that question, bit by bit.

"DIAGNOSE"

This is probably the most troublesome part of this question because it reiterates one of the biggest contributors to misunderstanding and poor mental health for people regarding their gender: the idea that being transgender is a mental disorder.

You can't diagnose someone with any gender because for that to happen, we would need several things: (1) A scientific understanding of what gender is and where it comes from that is agreed upon by specialists in the field; (2) A tool for consistently and accurately "measuring" one's gender; and (3) A standard definition of "transgender" (or any "gender") that is accurate, universal, and agreed upon by specialists in the field.

We don't have any of those things. Gender is a muddy subject that has scientists and theorists locked in a seemingly unending debate. Due to this muddiness, we don't have any sort of a test to measure someone's gender in a universal, accurate way (e.g., like the test we have for diabetes). The definitions of what it means to be transgender, genderqueer, man, woman, or any other gender identity are constantly in flux—and have been since forever.

All this goes to say that "diagnose" is a terrible word choice for this question. "Guess" would be a better one, but it still leads to the same shortcomings in the rest of the question.

"SOMEONE"

Someone, here, can usually be interpreted as "someone I don't really know that well," "someone I just met," or "someone I saw on the bus." In all cases, the "someone" describes a person with whom the asker does not have an open, personal relationship, and that's the key problem: people with whom you have an open, personal relationship are the only people whose gender you can [somewhat] accurately guess.

Though I would still recommend against it.

When people ask about "diagnosing someone's" gender, it's generally for one of two reasons: they aren't sure what pronouns to use around that person, or they're just plain curious. If it's only the former, there's an easy solution to that dilemma in the next paragraph. If it's only the latter, you should keep your curiosity in check. Gender is a personal thing, and while you might not think there's any harm in asking a stranger "Are you transgender?" that's because there wouldn't be, if it were the *only* time a transgender person were ever asked that. But that's not how it works, and the questions asked of transgender people aren't always that politely phrased (e.g., "What do your genitals look like?").

If you aren't sure what pronouns to use for a person, simply ask them. A good way to ask this question isn't "Are you a boy or a girl?" but rather "What are your preferred gender pronouns?" This is a great question to get in the habit of asking in general, and one that will make the gender-diverse people in your life way more comfortable being in your life.

"AS TRANSGENDER"

Transgender is, as you likely know by now, an incredibly broad term. It's generally used as an umbrella term under which many different gender identities are sheltered, all grouped by the commonality of being "non-cisgender identities." So "diagnosing someone as transgender" is about as much of an insight into who they are as "diagnosing someone as cisgender."

> DRILL: For the next few days, when referring to cisgender people in conversation (e.g., "Then my friend Jim said...") add the descriptor "cisgender" (e.g., "Then my cisgender friend Jim said..."). If you don't normally do this, it will likely be a bit uncomfortable—and will raise eyebrows—but embrace it. It'll help you internalize the issues of "otherness" and marginalization regarding transgender people, as well as highlight the ineffectiveness of that label in providing helpful additional information about a person.

I bring this up because it hits at the crux of why the central question of this chapter is a problem: because many times when we ask if someone is "transgender" what we are really asking is if they are "different," "other," "non-cisgender," or at its worst, if they are abnormal, weird, or broken.

Being transgender means being marginalized, and that marginalization is never as apparent as when we attempt to sum up a person as "other." A "normal" person is described and viewed in the myriad ways that make them unique (e.g., "Jim is my friend who is a twenty-year-old engineering student who likes riding ponies.") because describing them with the labels one can assume ("Jim is a cisgender man") sates no curiosity. An "other" person can be simply described using their "otherness" (e.g., "Jim is my transgender friend.").

What to ask instead

The next time you hear yourself wondering whether someone is transgender, or what gender a person is, ask *yourself* the following questions instead.

Do I need to know if this person is transgender?

Yes.

No.

Why?

Cuz I'm curious.

To know what pronouns to use.

Ask them what pronouns they prefer.

Stay outta their Kool-Aid!

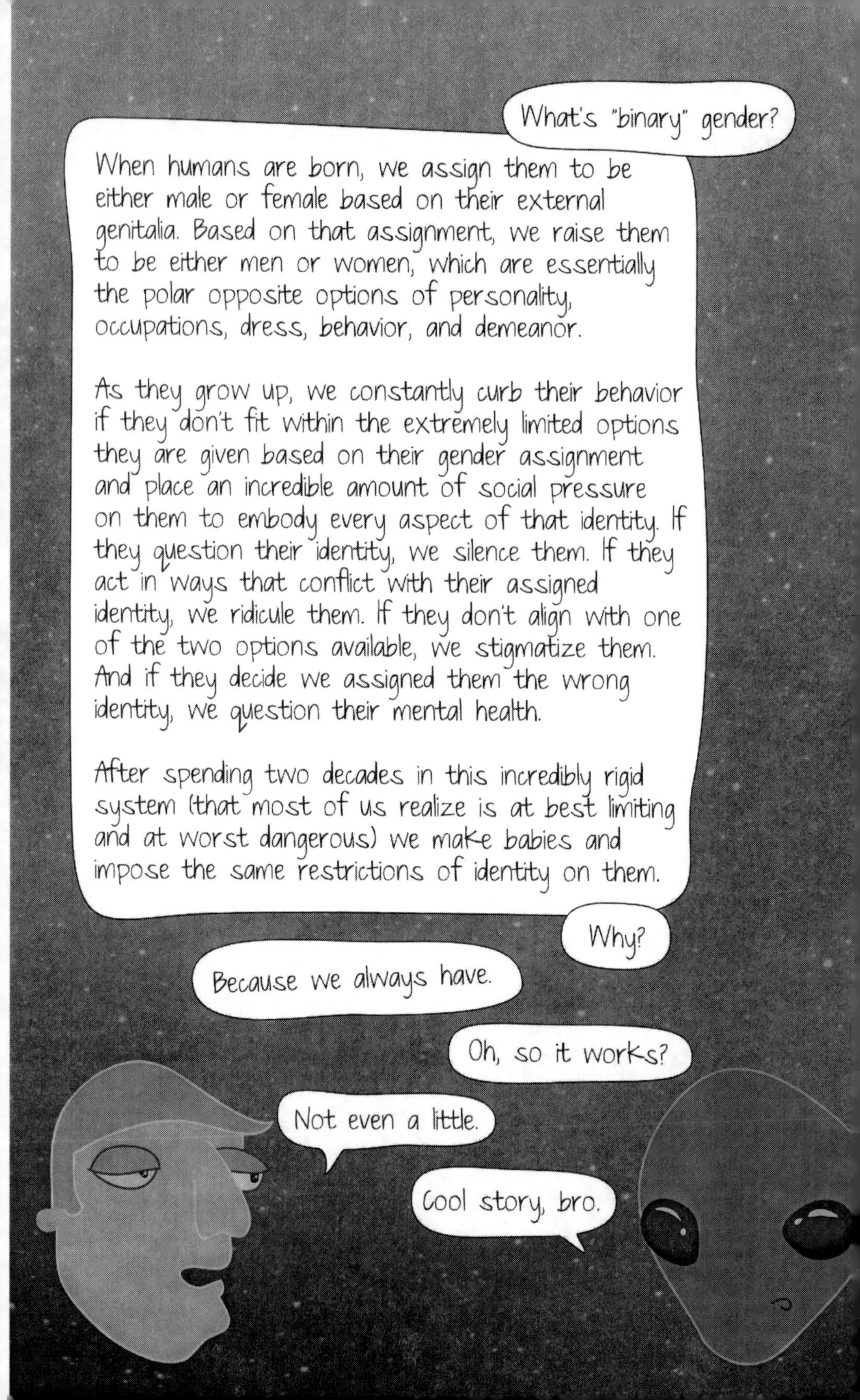

CHAPTER 19

THE DANGERS OF NORMALIZED BINARY GENDER

TO BE YOURSELF IN A WORLD THAT IS CONSTANTLY TRYING TO MAKE YOU SOMETHING ELSE IS THE GREATEST ACCOMPLISHMENT.

—*Ralph Waldo Emerson*

When we think about the gender binary, it's common for our minds to go in one of two directions: we think of the folks who "fit" into and are supported by the binary options (typically, cisgender people), or we think of folks who don't "fit" and experience hardship as a result of the binary options (typically, trans* people). The gender binary leads to dichotomous thinking—who'd'a thunk?

Relying on a gender-diverse, spectrum-based understanding of identity, I want to explore the potentially negative effects the gender binary has on most people, not just self-identified trans* folks.

Let's start by establishing a common definition for some specific terms I will be using in this chapter:

Binary Gender: a system of gender with only two options (here: woman or man)

Dissonance: an uncomfortable sense of confusion, or a lack of harmony, between one's individual identity and their cultural identity

Normalized: reinforced by society through social norms

EXPLAINING THE BINARY GENDER SYSTEM TO AN ALIEN

How would you explain the gender binary, and all of its implications, to an alien (what a galactocentric term!) who just landed on Earth? Fun idea! Here's how I would do it:

"When humans are born, we assign them to be either male or female based on their external genitalia. Based on that assignment, we raise them to be either men or women, which are essentially the polar opposite options of personality, occupations, dress, behavior, and demeanor.

"As they grow up, we constantly curb their behavior if they don't fit within the extremely limited options they are given based on their gender assignment and place an incredible amount of social pressure on them to embody every aspect of that identity. If they question their identity, we silence them. If they act in ways that conflict with their assigned identity, we ridicule them. If they don't align with one of the two options available, we stigmatize them. And if they decide we assigned them the wrong identity, we question their mental health.

"After spending two decades in this incredibly rigid system—that most of us realize is at best limiting and at worst dangerous—we make babies and impose the same restrictions of identity on them."

Alien: "Why?"

Me: "Because we always have."

Alien: "Oh. So it works?"

Me: "Not even a little."

Alien: "Cool story, bro."

THE GENDER BINARY WORKS "NOT EVEN A LITTLE"

Let's consider the best-case example for the gender binary, an imaginary person I am making up named Jack Jackson.

Jack was born with a penis and testicles, labeled male at birth, raised to be a boy, and has never once questioned that assignment. He is naturally athletic, aggressive, domineering, physically strong, emotionally reclusive, loves working with his hands, and doesn't cry even when he gets a really bad splinter (like, size of a toothpick under the fingernail bad). His jaw and brow are as pronounced as his shoulders are wide. He feels comfy in boots, blue jeans, and a slightly dirty plaid shirt; has never trimmed any hairs but the ones on his head (which he keeps at a standard 1" length, unstyled); speaks in a low voice; prefers logic over sentiment; and once killed a grizzly bear with a knife while riding bareback on another grizzly bear.

DRILL: Create your own character who is a hyperbole of a male as dictated by societal expectations of maleness (like my Jack Jackson), and do the same for a character who is a hyperbole of femaleness (Jill Jillson?).

Jack Jackson is everything that is the binary idea of "man." Even his name says man...twice. So how does the binary hurt him?

Because even for Jack, who experiences no dissonance between his internal identity and the binary option he was assigned, the binary gender system isn't just a lens we use when we look internally, but one we use when we examine other people. The odds of Jack finding satisfaction in a romantic partner (another "perfect" man or woman) or friend are extremely slim. Having a binary expectation of people in your life constantly leads to people in your life falling short: they either aren't woman enough or man enough, and in either case they are at least somewhat inadequate.

Further, Jack is going to gauge his interactions with others based on his assessment of which binary gender they are, because both options bring with them an incredibly specific set of how-to instructions. When things don't go well with treating individuals based on the prescriptions the gender binary has provided him, he's going to be miffed, but he'll be unable to explain that miffed-ness because dudes don't get miffed.

"I am Jack's miffed disposition. I get miffed. Jack ignores me. I eat Jack alive from the inside."

MOST MEN AREN'T JACK, AND MOST WOMEN AREN'T JILL

Even for people who absolutely align with every aspect of their binary gender option, the binary doesn't work because they have to interact with others who don't align. But most of us don't align absolutely, and this is where we start to experience dissonance.

Dissonance happens in varying degrees. It's not the yes/no picture we often paint it to be (are we starting to sense a theme yet?). You can (and likely do) experience some dissonance as a result of your gender even if you don't consider yourself to be trans*.

DRILL: Make a list of all the expectations of you based on your gender identity that you don't live up to or embody. Now, make a list of all the expectations of another gender identity (not your gender) that you do live up to or embody. The completed list is one way of assessing your gender dissonance.

For some people, the dissonance they experience is so mellow it's something they don't realize until they're asked about it—until they realize it's an option to experience dissonance. I have had conversations with plenty of people about this idea, and it's amazing how relieving it is for some people when they realize it's more "normal" (my language) to not fully identify with their normalized gender. Here's a story from a friend (an actual friend, not like an *I need advice, but it's for a friend* "friend") who experienced mild dissonance growing up:

"It was like when there is a word on the tip of your tongue, but you can't think of it. You know it's there, but you don't know exactly what it is. But you feel pressure to get it out, to say it—almost anxiety. Then, when we first talked about what gender really is, it was like the word finally came to me, all these years later.

"I always felt friction—friction with my family, my dad, my brother, my friends, myself. I never felt completely comfortable, and it just felt like something was off. In hindsight, I think it's because I was never the most boyish of boys. At the time, it felt like there was something wrong with me. Or that was just how all teenagers were. I had no idea it was a gender thing."

This experience, or a version of it, is something a lot of people are able to relate to. You might call it "growing pains," "teenage awkwardness," "[something hormoney]," or something else, but what it all boils down to is experiencing and coping with identity dissonance: being told you're one thing and knowing on the inside you aren't that. If you're not 100 percent whatever you're being told you are supposed to be, you've likely experienced some dissonance. And the less you are whatever it is you're "supposed" to be, the more severe your dissonance will be.

At its worst, giving people just two polar-opposite options for gender based on their sex and forcing them into one of the two can lead to extreme levels of dissonance, depression, anxiety, and self-harm. Here's a story from a person about his daily experience with his gender identity and female body (warning: this story contains suicidal ideations and self-harm):

"I most feel like I don't fit into the gender I was assigned when I am using the bathroom, or any time I am near a mirror. I hate seeing my body. My female features in my face can't be hidden, and they always make me uncomfortable, but that's not even the worst. It's the rest of my female body. I try to never see myself naked, because when I do I hate myself the most. In my worst moments, I have taken a knife to my breasts, crying, threatening myself, wanting to be dead, before collapsing."

A LOT OF PEOPLE AREN'T JACK OR JILL

Beyond the mild to severe dissonance binary-identified folks may experience not being Jack enough or Jill enough, there is a whole group of people we're overlooking: folks who don't see themselves as Jack or Jill.

For some of these people, a normalized binary is restrictive because they don't see themselves aligning with either option but as more of a combination of both. And for others, they may see themselves as a third option altogether. Some folks who fit into these groups may use labels for themselves such as "non-binary," "bigender," "genderfluid," "neutrois," "third-gender," something else, or—hold onto your hats—they may simply stick with the labels they were assigned and identify as "man" or "woman."

We all cope with dissonance experienced from fitting into the gender binary differently. It feels like there are new labels popping up every month that are, in many ways, people trying to find ways to cope with this. For some people, they externalize their dissonance and attach themselves to a label group that most closely describes their experience, and in that they find comfort and support. For others, this is an internal experience, and while they may simply identify as "woman" or "man," they may internally have a completely different idea of what that means from the normalized definition we all share.

But ultimately, what this all spells out is that a lot of people, for a lot of different reasons, aren't Jack or Jill, but they live in a world where they are being told again and again and again that they are.

I GOT 99 PROBLEMS AND NORMALIZED BINARY GENDER IS MOST OF THEM

Would it be a reductive way to view complex social issues to say that moving beyond the gender binary would lead to a far happier society, like adding a pile of kittens to any person lying in a bed? Yes. It would.

It'd be impossible to know unless we tried it. But you've probably never had a pile of kittens added to you while you were lying in bed, yet (barring allergies or kitten-related trauma histories) we can probably agree that would be just plain delightful.

What I can say with certainty is that moving beyond a binary understanding of gender on the individual level can be an incredibly liberating, life-and-self-affirming, stress-relieving experience. It will help you have more healthy expectations for yourself and others in your life. It's like opening up a pressure valve that's been building your entire life. Even if there was just a little pressure in there, it's still a relief to let it out.

Two options for gender is too few. There are seven billion individuals on this earth. We owe ourselves at least that many choices for how to be a person.

CHAPTER 20

A "NON-VITAL" MEDICAL PROCEDURE

SOME PEOPLE SEE THE GLASS HALF FULL. OTHERS SEE IT HALF EMPTY. I SEE A GLASS THAT'S TWICE AS BIG AS IT NEEDS TO BE.

—*George Carlin*

For a lot of folks who are trans*, sexual reassignment surgery (SRS, now often being called "Gender Confirmation Surgery" due to its more positive connotations) or hormone therapy (depending on the age of the person) are medical interventions that can allow their minds to align with their bodies in a way they've never experienced, a way that most cisgender people take for granted.

This is still considered a controversial topic by many. It's rarely covered by health insurance, is exceedingly expensive, and is viewed by many critics to be "elective" or "non-vital" surgery, the same way one might view a cosmetic rhinoplasty.

As I was publishing this book, a scandal covered by the media focused on this particular issue. The way it was covered was problematic—as is usually the case when things of this nature are covered—but it brought about a few realizations for me that helped to inform this chapter and will hopefully help you have a better understanding of SRS and transgender health.

Let me give you a rundown of how these situations often pan out and how SRS is viewed and then present a metaphor for a different method of understanding.

THE SITUATION

A trans* person says they need money for SRS and chooses to raise money using a crowdfunding platform or via donations from friends and family. The former option, crowdfunding, is becoming an ever more popular method of raising money for SRS, due to the popularity and success of crowdfunding platforms like Indiegogo.

THE ARGUMENTS MADE

The argument I keep seeing in the media, in discussion boards, and in forums is that this is an elective, "non-vital" surgery and is tantamount to raising money for cosmetic surgery. People question the ethics of raising money, stating that SRS is something the trans* person "needs" because it unfairly tugs at emotional heartstrings.

As I've seen it said many times, "A vital procedure is something you cannot live without, like an organ transplant," or in other words, "If you don't get SRS, your body will continue to work, even if your identity is 'misaligned' within it."

THE METAPHOR

Let's consider for a few moments a procedure not many (if any) would consider "elective" or "non-vital": a liver transplant. Liver transplants are a solution for liver failure or disease. We all have livers (and only one!), and without livers none of us would be able to live. Mind you, I'm no hepatologist, and this book is not meant to stand in for medical consultation (happy, lawyers?), but I'm pretty sure all this is true.

This metaphor is off to an impressively strong start.

Liver transplants are risky procedures. If the liver donated to the patient isn't a match with the patient's body, the body can reject the transplant through a hyper-medical-jargon-sounding process called "transplant rejection." If the body rejects the organ, innumerable leukocytes (Latin for little liver-attacking jerks) will be created and will start destroying the liver.

Where am I going with this?

The liver is a vital organ required for a person to live a healthy life. Let's consider that a person's mind (in this case, their gender identity), though usually an abstract concept, is similarly a vital organ required for someone to live a healthy life. If you're not onboard with this analogy, allow me to quote one of our era's great neuroscientists, Morpheus, who said simply "The body cannot live without the mind."

OK. So the mind is a vital organ. Listen to Morpheus. He showed you the door. Now let's walk through it.

What if someone is born with an organ that their body is slowly rejecting? In transplant terminology, we would call this "chronic rejection," something that happens constantly, slowly over time, with leukocytes engaged in a never-ending battle, eventually deteriorating the organ completely. We would consider transplanting that organ to be vital and would realize that the sooner we were able to do so, the more likely that person would be able to live a happy and healthy life.

The experience of being born with a gender identity that doesn't align with one's physical body is tantamount to being born with an organ that one's body is rejecting. In this case, rather than being white blood cells, the leukocytes are innumerable instances of socialization and microaggressions that say over and over again that the person's mind and body aren't a match, they are wrong, unhealthy, or broken. If this person doesn't receive a transplant, allowing their mind to find a body that it is a match with, the leukocytes (microaggressions) may eventually win their war, and we will lose our patient.

This is a pretty lurid metaphor, and a bit sensational, no? No.

In a 2012 study conducted by the Scottish Transgender Alliance, 84 percent of transgender people reported they had considered suicide. About half of them had attempted it. The social pressures and constant microaggressions that told these people their minds did not belong in their bodies (the leukocytes) prevailed. And society failed.

Now to be clear, I am not saying SRS would have "cured" these people of their ailments and saved their lives. What I am saying is that viewing SRS as a non-vital medical intervention, instead of viewing it with the same respect we hold for a liver transplant, is part of the problem.

WHAT'S THE SOLUTION?

If we want to care for the health of trans* people who are experiencing the mind and body dysphoria I described in the metaphor as similar to transplant rejection (note: this is not to say this is how all—or even most—trans* people experience their gender but is rather a particular type of dysphoria some trans* people may experience), I see two clear options:

One, and this one is my preference, we can create a society that no longer exerts the social pressures and microaggressions that lead to this level of unhealthy dysphoria, a society in which individuals' minds will always match their bodies because we take individuals as individuals and don't attempt to force them into molds they weren't born for. And all this happens…now!

Or two, we understand that SRS and hormone therapy are procedures that allow a person to be healthy in a way they may never be healthy otherwise, and we find ways to support individuals in pursuing these treatments, hold the treatments in the same esteem and with the same "vital" gravity as organ transplants, and push our medical institutions and insurance companies to do the same.

SRS can be a complicated conundrum, but it doesn't have to be. A lot of people view it pessimistically, others view it optimistically, but it can be simply what it is: a medical treatment to help a person get healthy.

CHAPTER 21

A UNIFIED UNDERSTANDING OF GENDER

SOMETIMES THE THING THAT BRINGS US TOGETHER ALSO PULLS US APART. SORT OF LIKE A ZIPPER.

—*Jarod Kintz*

Let's review.

Gender is a cultural construction. The labels we have for gender identities are essentially a means of classifying personality, with a misinformed importance put on physical characteristics people are born with. And if people don't identify with one of the two main gender identity options—specifically, the one they were assigned at birth based on their physical characteristics—they will have a tougher life than those who do.

But we know it's not that simple.

Gender is like a Rubik's Cube with one hundred squares per side, and every time you twist it to take a look at another angle, you make it that much harder a puzzle to solve. A normal Rubik's Cube is tough enough; a one-hundred-squares-per-side cube is indecipherable. Your best bet may seem to be to just leave it as it came from the factory and enjoy the uniformity of the pretty colors on each side.

Unless you break the rules.

The conventional way to solve a Rubik's Cube is, without question, the most cumbersome. My brother and I developed an infatuation for Rubik's Cubes many years ago. We both mastered the 3 X 3 cube quickly, but the 4 X 4 gave me a run for my money. When I wasn't feeling particularly clever, I would dismantle it into its fifty-seven fundamental pieces and rebuild it as a completed puzzle. So pretty. So simple. Sam Killermann: 1; Ernő Rubik: 0.

Maybe we're approaching the gender puzzle wrong.

A lot of the toughest questions that used to keep me up at night are based on our current understanding of gender, with answers (if they're even answerable) that may or may not modify that current understanding. These are questions like "Why do so many cultures have only two genders?" "How would a society without a gender taxonomy work?" and "Why am I not allowed to wear halter tops when they make my shoulders look so good?"

Attempting to understand gender by modifying our basic understanding of gender is like attempting to solve the puzzle using the rules given to us—twisting and pivoting and rotating this one-hundred-sided cube, hoping we'll have a breakthrough. One night, a couple years ago, when I wasn't feeling particularly clever, I thought maybe it'd be best if we just took the whole thing apart and rebuilt it as a completed puzzle.

Then I realized something that changed the way I looked at gender.

IT'S MORE ABOUT THE PIECES THAN IT IS ABOUT THE PUZZLE

Bartenders will tell you that if you have a favorite mixed drink at a particular bar, and you want to ensure you're able to enjoy that drink elsewhere, you should ask the bartender how it's made, not what it's called. Sorry. You're not going to be able to order your Screaming Pelvis in Ft. Lauderdale. But if you know the ingredients, the relative amount of each, and the process that goes into making a Screaming Pelvis, you can tell those things to the bartender and your pelvis can scream with no geolocative restraint.

I've had conversations with thousands of individuals about their gender. I have read a ton about gender in general, both in "peer-reviewed" journals and "peer-bashed-in-comments-section" blog posts. I know most of the big theories, and I know most of the science. And for the longest time I tried to synthesize all of that information and reconcile it with my own gender experience—to make it all make sense—until I decided I was looking at it all wrong.

Every person I've talked to (no hyperbole: *every* person) has had a different take on gender. Like a specialty drink, sometimes these different takes were as minor as the relative amount of each ingredient ("My Screaming Pelvis has two parts tequila to one part hot sauce"), but sometimes the ingredients were different altogether ("Who puts hot sauce in their Screaming Pelvis?"). The majority of these people were self-identified cisgender women or men, but a hugely disproportionate amount were self-identified within the transgender umbrella. When you read about gender, you get a similarly diverse take on what gender is. The only thing most people seem to agree upon is that they have gender, but even that's not a universal theory.

So riddle me this: what merit does the label "man" have if it means different things to different people, and what criteria do I need to meet in order to identify myself with that label?

Further, for someone to self-identify as non-binary, how much do they need to not identify with one of the binary options? That is, what're the thresholds at which a person goes from "I'm a woman," to "I'm a bit butch, but still a woman," to "I'm not a woman or a man, but something in between," to "I'm neither man nor woman, but I'm intrigued by this Screaming Pelvis you keep talking about."

Or, going back to the metaphor, how many ingredients can someone omit or add to a drink before it stops being a Screaming Pelvis and becomes something else altogether? (A round of Laughing Rectums, anyone?)

How far away from the societal definition of "man" can I be before I should start considering another label (e.g., "genderqueer") to describe myself?

WE'RE ALL A BIT GENDERQUEER, AND NONE OF US ARE GENDERQUEER

Writing that is one of the scarier things I've ever done, because I realize it takes me from being this "Accessibility matters! Everyone should be able to understand gender!" type of person, to a "Down with society! Everything is a lie! There is no spoon!" type of person. I promise I'm not nearly interesting enough to be the second person. This idea isn't actually that radical at all. Give me a moment to explain. Then we can spoon.

From biggest picture to smallest picture, any understanding of gender we have is, at best, flawed. We know there are only two types of people on Earth: men and women. But we know that there are more than men and women: there's also "other." But we know that we can't just divide the globe into men, women, and other because gender varies from continent to continent, country to country, region to region. But we can't just say that this region has men, women, and other because even within regions, gender varies among ethnicities. And economic classes. And age groups. But we also can't say that all people in a particular region of the same ethnicity, economic class, and age group will be either man, woman, or other because each person's embodiment of gender varies slightly.

In other words, we know one thing: we don't know anything.

At worst, we have "There are 7 billion people on this planet, and they can all be adequately grouped into one of two categories." And on the other end, we have "There are 7 billion people on this planet who all have individual identities, but we still group most of them into one of two categories." Both of these options, and every option in between, are flawed. What I'm suggesting is a third option.

What if we consider that the binary understanding of gender we have, the one that a vast majority of people identify with, is really more about threshold than it is about identity?

Earlier, I said it's impossible to "diagnose someone as transgender" because, for one reason (of many), we don't have a tool for measuring gender. Let's use our imaginations and pretend such a tool exists.

The simplest (and most non-magic-dependent) way I can imagine such a tool working would be a test where people self-identify with gendered traits, descriptors, and characteristics. There would be a huge list of things, half of them attributes of man-ness, masculinity, and male-ness and the other half attributes of woman-ness, femininity, and female-ness, but they wouldn't be labeled such. The prompt would simply be "Check all that describe you."

Now, the question I'll pose to you is what percentage of the man-ness, masculinity, and male-ness options does a binary-identified "man" need to check to consider himself a man? All of them? 90 percent for an A? 70 percent, like what you need for a college degree? 51 percent, for a majority of mannitude? Or perhaps more importantly, how many of the woman-ness, femininity, and female-ness options is he allowed before he's disqualified?

My experience tells me that if such a test were made, our understanding of "genderqueer" might be turned on its head. Right now we think of roughly 1 to 3 percent of the population as trans* and the rest as cisgender, binary, or "normal." If everyone were to take our imaginary test, I'd be surprised if even 1 percent of people were 100 percent in either of the binary options. And even if they were, it'd be important to note that if you controlled for region, race, class, and age, we would all grade that test differently.

So if my theory is true, that would mean we're all a bit genderqueer. And if that were true, that would mean that none of us are really genderqueer—because queerness ceases to be queer if it's the norm.

Meaning we're all a bit genderqueer, and none of us are genderqueer.

F.Y.I. in case you're wondering, I'm in the process of making that imaginary tool much less imaginary, and by the time this book is published, I will hopefully be pilot-testing the prototype.

SO IS EVERYTHING A LIE? IS THERE A SPOON OR NOT?

What I'm suggesting here, Neo, is more about changing the way we look at things and less about changing what things are. Your gender hasn't changed. The world hasn't changed. You're still you. The world is still the world.

If we reconsider the semantics—the labels we use to unite and divide ourselves—of gender and realize that they aren't concrete and well defined but rather amorphous and more about degrees of alignment than categories, we will erase the stigma attached to non-binary and trans* gender identities.

I'm arguing that we're more alike than we are different and that the degree of "otherness" between a particular binary-gender person and a particular non-binary person may not be any more different than the degrees of difference between one particular woman and another woman.

And I'm arguing that we're more different than we are alike and that your identity may be more closely aligned with a particular person who identifies with a different identity than you than with a particular person who is a member of your identity group.

I am hoping this understanding can lead to empathy (if you're more the emotional type) and cognitive complexity (if you're more the logical type).

I am hoping you can experience empathy for others that is not amplified or guided by your alignment with their gender identity but driven by the fact that we're all gendered people composed of different combinations of similar ingredients.

And I am hoping you can embrace cognitive complexity and realize gender is not either/or in most cases but both/and; I'm suggesting you realize that the black and white only exist when folks are only given two options, and that most people are different thresholds of gray when considered on an individual level.

Above all, I want you know that after all this, I am totally down for a round of Screaming Pelvises.

Pelvisii?

FEMINISM &

GENDER

EQUITY

feminists   people feminists   misogynists
call misogynists

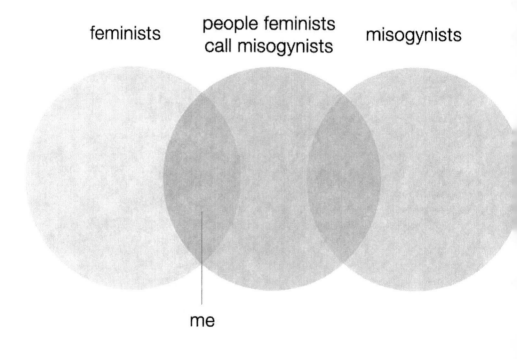

me

CHAPTER 22

MY EXPERIENCE WITH FEMINISM

I MYSELF HAVE NEVER BEEN ABLE TO FIND OUT PRECISELY WHAT FEMINISM IS. I ONLY KNOW THAT PEOPLE CALL ME A FEMINIST WHENEVER I EXPRESS SENTIMENTS THAT DIFFERENTIATE ME FROM A DOORMAT.

—*Rebecca West*

Feminism is, to many people, a loaded word packed with negative connotations. When I was first introduced to the concept, it was through a less-than-positive manner, but it's just the first part of a long story that ends with me, now, proudly wearing the "feminist" badge.

THE STORY OF THE WELL-INTENTIONED MISOGYNIST

I'm a misogynist. I am quite sure of this fact because of how many times I've been told so. I've been told so in comments on my website, responses to my comments on other folks' websites, indirectly by speakers at conferences, and in a few occasions, directly to my face.

And as the old saying goes: if it looks like a duck and quacks like a duck, it probably hates women.

I Remember the First Time I Learned I Was a Misogynist

I was a bright-eyed college freshman auditing a gender studies (read: women's issues) class at Purdue University. In a class discussion about objectification of women, I asked, quite earnestly (read:

naïvely), "Why is it bad for me to say 'Jessica Alba is super hot'—I mean, isn't she?"

In the discussion (read: crucifiction) that followed, I was called a misogynist by a few of my classmates and indirectly, by the professor. Ignorant to what that word meant but understanding via context clues it wasn't good, I shut up and did my best to make myself invisible for the remaining 50 minutes of class.

When I got back to my dorm, I immediately hopped on my computer and looked up the word. And much to my surprise, I learned that I hated women.

I Never Knew I Hated Women

I learned that I did from my classmates and professor the first time I was called a misogynist. If you had asked me a few hours before learning that what my feelings were towards women, I would have told you that I opposite-of-hated women.

I grew up in a two mom household. One of my moms was my biological mother, who regularly reminds me that she "grew me" so I need to listen to her. My other mom was my oldest sister, who didn't take much encouraging to fill the head-of-household role when my mom (the one who grew me) was working. Or not in the house. Or in the bathroom. Addie was bossy.

As a byproduct of this, I (apparently incorrectly assumed I) grew up with the utmost respect for women. Between my mom, my sister who pretended to be my mom, and my other older sister, I had plenty of positive female role models.

My mom worked miracles in a solo effort to keep us housed and fed. My sisters played sports, got solid grades, went to college, and never once got arrested for shoplifting (unlike my scumbag friends). And other than two men, all of the other positive figures in my life (teachers, a couple of neighbors) were women.

If anything, based on my mostly rocky experience with would-be male role models, one could even argue that I was inclined to be a misandrist. I would have been one of the people to argue that.

I Thought I Wanted To Support Women

This opposite-of-hatred I thought I held for women is what led me to check out that gender studies class my freshman year of college in the first place.

I started getting an inkling of what the term "oppression" meant, and word on the street was that all these women I thought I loved were members of one of the biggest groups being targeted by that nasty idea. I didn't like that, so I wanted to learn what I could do about it.

It was a shock and a relief when I learned that I didn't respect women, but in fact hated them, so I guess I didn't need to worry about remedying that oppression thing any more. That feminist thing was going to be a lot of work, and being a misogynist was so easy I didn't even know I was doing it.

Meet Me: A Misogynist-Labeled Feminist

Okay, enough of that writing from the perspective of a version of me from the perspective of those who've labeled me a misogynist.

That was exhausting. But it was necessary because I wanted to tell you a story that is unfortunately all too common - the story of the Well-Intentioned Misogynist - a semantic impossibility that plays out on a daily basis.

Like freshman me, a lot of people (regardless of gender identity) don't know what the word "misogynist" means. It's likely they've never even considered that a word like that is necessary, because they don't think there is such a thing (a person who hates half the people in the world).

And like freshman me, a lot of people (regardless of gender identity) who aren't up to speed on the ideas of gender-based privilege and systemic oppression, are packed full of misconceptions of how the world works.

They aren't aware of how gender (and surely, all the identities one possesses) shapes one's individual experience, often times in a limiting way. They don't realize that we've created and support systems that are, in the simplest sense, unfair.

And like freshman me, a lot of these people are incredibly well intentioned.

Many times when well-intentioned people express their incomplete (or inaccurate, ignorant, ill-conceived... pick your i-word) understanding of the world and the issues women face, instead of being educated, they are written off as misogynists and the discussion ends there. Or worse, the conversation moves in a direction of vilifying that person.

This happens in articles on feminist websites, in comment sections and forums, at women's issues conferences, and in rarer occasions, during in-person interactions.

Labeling someone a misogynist, sexist, racist, etc is incredibly loaded and should be used only after giving sufficient evidence and discussion (ie not after just one comment). Otherwise it will quickly make someone who's trying to learn (if stumbling at it) shut down and/or go on the defensive.

This is the story of the "Well-Intentioned Misogynist." And like I said early, it's told everyday and it's hurting our feminist cause.

It's Time We Start Telling a New Story

We need to start realizing that everyone is at different levels of understanding of social justice and feminist issues. We're all raised in a society and bombarded by messages from mass media that normalizes oppressive and exploitative norms.

Some people are exposed to feminist or progressive thinking that challenges the dominant culture but many aren't. Some folks who are exposed to it want to learn and some don't.

And for those that do, we need to meet folks where they are in order to help them learn, develop, and grow from there.

We need to start realizing that while creating an enemy in a misogynist (because certainly, intentionally hurtful misogynists do exist) can be affirming and create unity and strength within the feminist community, it can also create apprehension in in prospective members who are ignorant but wanting to learn.

So before jumping to the conclusion that you're talking to a misogynist because they made a sexist comment, try sharing with them in a non-judgmental way why that comment was hurtful even if it is normalized in our society.

You just might be surprised at how open-minded they are.

CALLING PEOPLE MISOGYNISTS ISN'T HELPING FEMINISM

I'm called "misogynist" less and less as time passes and I learn how to be a proper feminist, but, as I mentioned before, when I first started wading into these waters I was errantly labeled a misogynist on a regular basis.

To say it was discouraging is to say cheesecake is "tasty." Cheesecake is freaking delicious.

As a feminist, I regularly find myself reading an article or a comment and having the knee-jerk reaction in my mind "this guy's a misogynist."

But I do my best to leave it at just that—a thought in my mind.

Let me tell you why, and introduce you to two ideas that might be new, but will likely strike you as "I think I already knew that" once you read them.

A Rose By Any Other Name Wouldn't Be a Rose

Labeling theory has been fostered and developed since the origins of sociology and really gained prominence in the 60s. There is a ton you can read about the idea, but I am going to crudely sum it up (for the sake of my argument in this article) in a few core points:

1. We, as a culture, create a system of "do"s and "don't"s that are informally taught to people as they mature and reinforced through social interaction and sanctions.

2. As social creatures, human beings derive a lot of what becomes us from our interactions with others.

3. If someone is labeled as a deviant (for breaking our cultural rules in #1) they are likely to internalize that label and continue (or begin) acting in that deviant way (because of #2).

Example: If you label a young person a criminal, that young person is likely to become an adult criminal.

The Person Is Not the Problem, The Problem Is the Problem

Externalization therapy is a practice developed by an Australian psychotherapist named Michael White. Again, there is much and more you can read about White and his work, but I want to give you the jist of this idea in a few points:

1. It's important to understand that an individual and the behav-

ior an individual participates in can be viewed as independent concepts.

2. Separating individuals and their destructive behavior (i.e., externalizing their behavior) is important in helping them move through it to positive behavior.

3. Re-focusing conversations in a way that makes a clear distinction between an individual and their behavior is one way to accomplish this positive development.

Example: Instead of labeling a youth as a criminal, explain that an instance of their behavior was a crime and reinforce the fact that a majority of the behavior they engage in is not.

My Humble Request: Think Twice Before Calling Someone a Misogynist

Every time we call someone a misogynist, there's a good chance we're creating a roadblock on our path to gender equity and social justice. How is this happening?

One, calling people misogynists means they are more likely to continue being (or become) a misogynist. Labeling theory has taught us that people internalize the labels they are given and are more likely to act in ways that support that label after being labeled that way. Label! (Sorry, couldn't resist)

And two, calling people misogynists encourages them to internalize their misogynistic behavior and internalized behavior is tough to change. Externalization therapy has taught us that if you are trying to help people change behavior, we need to do our best to help folks separate their behavior from their self. To do this, we need to change our conversation from talking about "misogynists" to "people who engage in misogynistic behavior." Finally, creating an enemy out of misogynists inspires those so-called misogynists to create an enemy out of feminists.

There's some interesting (and controversial) social-psych research that shows clearly defining an enemy can help strengthen a group and inspire action. This would be a great reason to support the use of the label misogynist (as it's an obvious, and powerful enemy for us to create), if relationships weren't reciprocal. They are. Creating a strong "Feminists against Misogynists" community, also creates a strong "Misogynists against Feminists" community. Not helpful.

What Can We Do Instead?

My mother taught me "if you don't have anything nice to say, don't say anything at all." But that's absurd. I don't think we should not say anything at all. We should definitely point out negative or destructive behavior and thinking and explain why those actions are sexist in a civil tone. But we shouldn't call the person a misogynist and make them wrong as a human being.

By avoiding labeling a person and using intentional effort to practice language that separates them from their misogynistic actions, we'll have a much better chance at helping them move into a greater understanding of gender issues.

And with luck, we'll have a new ally instead of a hardened enemy.

Translation: I didn't know we were allowed to order cosmos. Damnit. If I had known -- no! Screw this! Not fair. Time to be an asshole.

CHAPTER 23

A GENDER-INCLUSIVE FEMINIST PERSPECTIVE

THE WORD FEMINISM NEEDS TO BE TAKEN BACK. IT NEEDS TO BE RECLAIMED IN A WAY THAT IS INCLUSIVE OF MEN.

— *Annie Lennox*

Feminism is a multi-faceted, deeply-segmented movement. If you ask five feminists "What is feminism?" there is a good chance you'll get five different responses. There are some feminists who think feminism means working toward gender equity for everyone. I'm one of those feminists. But that's not a universal sentiment.

There are some feminists who believe that trans* people shouldn't be included in the feminism movement; some feminists see feminism as a means for retribution against men, a payback of sorts for innumerable years of male oppression; some feminists want to do away with gender and gender roles altogether; others don't; and some people think "feminist" is just another way of saying "lesbian" (those people are usually delightful to meet in person).

This isn't a book about all the types of feminism, and I wouldn't be the right person to write such a book. But this is a book about gender and my general theme is one of working toward equity for people of all genders. And I don't feel comfortable writing about that without reconciling how feminism can (and, in my opinion, should) play an integral part in achieving that goal.

WHY DO WE NEED FEMINISM?

While there aren't a ton of things all feminists agree on, there is one thing: the world is socially organized in a way that it's easier to be a man than it is to be any other gender. Remember that list of male privileges you read? This is that.

Feminism has been working to lessen the severity of male privilege since a long time ago in a galaxy not so far, far away. Feminism has been responsible for key achievements like women's right to own property (rather than, well, being property) and vote. These are great things for the gender equity movement.

Another way of putting all this is to say that feminism works to dismantle the patriarchy. Unfortunately, this way of putting it usually brings to mind a *"Les Miserables*, flag-waving, down with the government, all men are evil" brand of feminism, but this doesn't have to be the case.

DISMANTLING PATRIARCHY IS GOOD FOR EVERYONE

On its surface, patriarchy (men having absolute power) may seem like a good thing for men. I'll give you that. But, as we've discussed, the label "men" is a less than flawless way to describe half the people in the world. Because it's easy to understand why dismantling patriarchy would be good for other genders, let me focus here on how this will benefit men.

While it's hard to argue that things aren't better for men in society right now, things are far from perfect. There are a lot of societal problems that acutely affect men: men are less likely to graduate from college, and much less likely to continue education post-grad than women; men are more likely to be victims and perpetrators of crime, especially violent crime; due to this, men are disproportionately represented in the criminal justice system; men are more likely to experience clinical anxiety and depression; due to this and other compounding factors, men are far more likely to take their own lives.

What does any of this have to do with patriarchy?

All of this can be explained as being a byproduct of patriarchy, or, specifically, the socialization of men that is dictated in a patriarchal society. Patriarchy sets up a series of strict and unrealistic expectations for all men. It says men should be aggressive and not submissive; men should take charge and not take no for an answer; men are smarter and better than women; and showing emotion or weakness is a lowering yourself to the level of women, and forbidden.

The unrealistic and unhealthy expectations set forth for men in a patriarchal society, one that reinforces a gender binary and gender hierarchy, can be just as destructive for men as it is for individuals of any gender.

Dismantling "male" power can be as empowering to men as it is to others

Removing the expectations for men to be dominant and in power, as well as opening up access to those attributes to people of all genders, results in a society where people are empowered to be themselves, and not forced into certain roles or to possess certain attributes as a result of their gender.

People who want to fill roles with social power can do so and experience no dissonance in doing so. And people who do not want power can live a life without power. Which is great for them, assuming they don't want to hoverboard on water because "hoverboards don't work on water... unless you've got power!" (How's that for an obscure quote?)

LET'S TALK ABOUT THE WORD "FEMINISM"

"Is what I'm describing here really feminism?" you might be wondering. Or you might think "What you're talking about is humanism. I'm a humanist. Humanists are better than feminists because reasons." And it's possible all that's on your mind is "Did I have tacos for breakfast and lunch today?" Or maybe that's just me.

In any case, I'm a strong proponent for "feminism" (and an equally strong opponent against "humanism"–though I'm not anti-human, mind you), and I think the term already represents a gender-inclusive gender equity movement. All you have to do is think about the movement from a different perspective.

Dismantling patriarchy or affirming femininity

Patriarchy celebrates masculinity in its traditional sense, and pushes for a society where men are absolutely masculine, women are absolutely feminine, and that's all the people (Sorry, everyone else). In this line of thinking, the brunt of the negative impact of patriarchy could be considered to be a dichotomous look at gendered behavior, where masculinity (for men) is good, and femininity (in general) is bad.

Feminism can be (and is) a movement about affirming femininity in society. As feminists, we can argue that there is as much power and potential inherent in femininity as there is in masculinity, and that nobody should be chastised or disadvantaged for embodying aspects of femininity. For folks who don't identify internally with either femininity or masculinity, they can still experience the benefits of a society that doesn't hold masculinity as supreme.

Let's stop talking about the word "feminism" and start talking about gender equity

The other reason I'm pro "feminism" is because–and this is going to be blunt–I am quite fed up with all the in-group fighting, energy, and effort that's gone into debating "feminism" (the word, not the idea). I get similarly frustrated when I read an article on a feminist publication debating whether someone (e.g., Beyonce) is a "perfect feminist." Let me do everyone a favor: nobody is a perfect feminist, and "feminism" isn't a perfect label.

I vote for sticking with "feminism" because feminism has deep roots, is a recognizable movement, and–despite its faults–has done a lot for the betterment of people of all genders. But you don't have to agree with me. You can call yourself a Humanist, a Gender Equitist, or a Separatist, for all I care–as long as you're not a misogynist, I think we can focus our time and energy on working together to make things better for people of all genders.

Feminism isn't a bad word and the less time we spend debating and discussing that and the more time we spend working toward a society where femininity isn't persecuted the happier I will be and the closer we will be to a society where people can be themselves and write run-on sentences.

Keep blowing them up. I want to fly away to a planet where the people are nice to each other.

CHAPTER 24

WHY PEOPLE BELIEVE FEMINISM HATES MEN

THE FEMINIST AGENDA IS NOT ABOUT EQUAL RIGHTS FOR WOMEN. IT IS ABOUT A SOCIALIST, ANTI-FAMILY POLITICAL MOVEMENT THAT ENCOURAGES WOMEN TO LEAVE THEIR HUSBANDS, KILL THEIR CHILDREN, PRACTICE WITCHCRAFT, DESTROY CAPITALISM, AND BECOME LESBIANS.

— *Pat Robertson*

Pat Robertson famously said those words in the '90s, and the sentiment still rings as true in the ears of many today. It's an understatement to say that feminism has a bad rap.

But feminism doesn't hate men.

So why do so many people think feminism = man-hating? Let's look at a few explanations for this fallacy.

BECAUSE SOME INDIVIDUAL FEMINISTS HATE MEN

Surprised to hear me say that? It's true. There's no point in avoiding it, so we might as well start with it. Just look around the Internet.

In thirty seconds on Google, I found plenty of articles written by feminists who are anti-men and a delightful collection of quotes featuring anti-men feminist sentiments (my favorite: "To call a man an animal is to flatter him; he's a machine, a walking dildo." Thanks for the gem, Valerie Solanas).

What I'm trying to say is you don't have to look very hard to find examples of "feminists" who hate men.

But there's a difference between "feminists" and "misandrists."

Ever heard the term misandrist? It's like misogynist but for hating men instead of women.

Yes, misandrist is a word. But feminist doesn't mean "person who hates men." Feminist means "person who believes people should have equitable places in society regardless of their gender."

Some feminists may be misandrists. I quoted one above. But it's by no means a criterion to join the club.

A portion does not equal the whole, even if that portion is really loud.

They're not even that loud but can seem so because antifeminists like to cherry pick quotes and ignore the much greater number of feminist writings, people, and organizations that say otherwise.

Some individual feminists hate men. A lot of feminists might hate men. You might even argue based on what you find on the Internet that most feminists hate men. It's irrelevant.

What matters is that feminism, distilled down to its absolute core, is about gender equity. The goal of feminism is to create a society in which individuals' genders don't restrict them from an equitable shot at success and happiness.

Most feminists actively disagree with the belief that women are better than men and think that feminists who are anti-men are going against the fundamental principles of feminism, which say we're all deserving and worthy human beings—women, men, trans*—and should be treated as such. So man-hating isn't a part of that goal. It's an unfortunate reactionary sentiment bought into by some people (misandrists) who also identify with the feminist movement.

A lot of people get drunk in college, but we know that college is more than a big drinking club, right? Isn't it? Maybe I attended the wrong college.

BECAUSE PEOPLE HAVE BEEN TOLD FEMINISTS HATE MEN FOR 200+ YEARS

The whole "feminists hate men" thing has been tossed around for quite a long time now. It's not new. The first "feminist" women who began advocating for equal status of women in the United States did so in the late 1700s, but it didn't really pick up steam until the late 1800s.

What crazy, radical things were these man-haters asking for? Primarily, the rights to own property, attend college, and vote.

In response to these requests, they were labeled as radical anti-family, anti-God, anti-men hedonists. That labeling has continued to today because—surprise!—a group with a lot of power (men) tends to do whatever it can to maintain that power (dismiss equal rights as radical).

It's happened with every oppressed ethnic group (from the Irish to the Africans) that's immigrated to the country. It happened with oppressed religious groups (from the Catholics to the Muslims), and it continues today with the oppressed gender group.

Why do people believe it if it's not true?

Because people are irrational. There are entire books presenting evidence of this (check out Sway for a great example). One way we act irrationally is called diagnosis bias.

A particularly fascinating study showed that the smallest change in the way you describe someone can completely alter the way you perceive their behavior. How about an example?

A university class (unknowing lab rats) had a substitute professor. To introduce the professor, the class members were given short bios. What they didn't know was that half the bios had been very slightly altered (e.g., exchanging warm, positive adjectives for cold, callous ones).

After the lecture, the students were asked to review the professor. The entire class saw the same man say the same things, yet the reviews were split 50/50 positive and negative. Half the class said he was personable, considerate, and engaged while the other half said he was ruthless, would do anything for success, and didn't care about students or people. The smallest change in the way someone is described can make a dramatic change in the way you interpret their behavior and demeanor.

Now, hypothetically speaking, imagine how twisted the perceptions would have been if the students were told the professor was a student-hating, self-serving, radical hedonist.

BECAUSE MOST MEN AREN'T BAD BUT THINK FEMINISM SAYS THEY ARE

Let me bust a few myths:

1. Being a feminist doesn't mean you believe "all men are rapists." This quote comes from a book by Marilyn French, and it seems to be recited more by antifeminists (as a means of debunking feminism) than by feminists themselves. It's simply a ridiculous statement that's been given a ridiculous amount of airtime.

2. Being a feminist doesn't mean you think all men are evil. Following up on the last point, a lot of antifeminist folks make the argument that feminists believe all men are evil. This is not true.

3. Being a feminist doesn't mean you blame every individual man you know for hundreds of years of oppressive behavior. Just like you wouldn't point at a random white person today and blame them for slavery, you can't blame an individual man today for a history of sexism.

A lot of people think about the things above, think about the men they know (or if they are men, they think about themselves), and think "That's ridiculous. _____ isn't an evil rapist who is responsible for hundreds of years of sexism."

A lot of people are right.

The thing feminism thinks is bad is the hundreds of years of sexism part, as well as the existence of sexism today. Sexism is the problem—sexism that a lot of men engage in and a lot of women internalize. Men engage in sexism because they've been taught to behave/think that way. Women internalize it for the same reason. Feminism asks both men and women to critically think about those normalized behaviors and their impact and holds people accountable to sexist thinking and behavior even if they didn't initially realize it was sexist.

So yes, it's natural to get defensive when someone brings up feminist issues because it's likely you never thought you were doing anything wrong. Does that make sexist behavior acceptable? No.

That's why we need to do a better job as a society to teach people how to treat each other with equity. That's what feminism is trying to do.

BECAUSE SOME FEMINISTS AREN'T WILLING TO ADDRESS MEN'S ISSUES

Working toward gender equity means equity for all genders, right? Then what about men? And what about trans* folks? This is a question that often gets raised by men (about men, not as much for trans* folk). Feminism in general has mixed feelings about addressing men's (and trans*) issues.

I'll be the first person to admit that there are a lot of gender-based men's issues to address. Like why young men today are less likely to graduate from college, attain a high GPA, be active in extracurricular organizations, or seek leadership roles; or why men in general have always been more likely to be caught up in the criminal justice system or be homeless. These are real issues, surely, and things our society should work to correct.

But do many feminists ignore these issues because they hate men?

No.

Their mixed feelings about addressing men's issues tend to stem from the fact that "men's issues" tends to be the default in our society. We're a male-dominant society. Many feminists are concerned that addressing men's issues (or gender issues as a broad goal) will move the conversation completely away from women's issues, resulting in no progress for the women's part of the gender progress. So instead they focus on women's issues and allow others to focus on other's issues. Many feminists would like to see pro-feminist men tackle men's issues in a way that doesn't blame women and feminism for all their problems (like many men's rights activists do).

However, it's worth noting that plenty of feminist publications and movements are both men- and trans*-inclusive. This is the type of feminism I personally support, the kind that takes an intersectional approach to feminism and looks at how different groups of genders, sexual orientations, races, classes, and more are dominated in our society.

BECAUSE SENSATIONALISM IS A GOOD WAY TO DISTRACT FROM REAL ISSUES

It's pretty messed up that being born a certain way means you're going to be less likely to earn as much money, achieve the same tier of success, be treated with respect and fairness, or be elected into political office, among other things, but those restrictions are objectively measurable.

Those issues mentioned above affect just about every identity group in the United States that is not white and male (and straight, nondisabled, etc.)—like me! Instead of dealing with inequality and giving up a bit of unearned power, it's far more fruitful to change the conversation and put the oppressed group on the defensive.

Blacks are more likely to be imprisoned because being a criminal is part of being black. Have fun arguing about that while we enjoy our unfairly granted "innocent" verdicts.

Gays can't be given rights to form families because being a child molester is part of being gay. Go ahead and re-read all of those nonsensical studies and commission some more while we enjoy our access to the 1,138 benefits granted solely to married couples.

Women don't earn as much as men because earning a lower wage for the same work is part of being a woman. Oh, and babies. Don't forget, you make the babies. What a miracle! That should be payment enough.

Social change is slow because the people in power are the ones writing the narrative, and they often choose a distracting narrative

Did you know that up until the early twentieth century there was an actual medical condition called "female hysteria" (yes, "hyster," as in hysterectomy, or pertaining to the uterus)?

Some of the symptoms of female hysteria: loss of appetite, nervousness, irritability, fluid retention, emotional excitability, outbursts of negativity, excessive sexual desire, and "a tendency to cause trouble."

In other words, if a woman wasn't eating, was eating too much, was angry, happy, wanted to have sex, or wanted equal rights for women (you trouble causers, you!), she was mentally ill and her behavior could be dismissed as such.

Guess who came up with that idea? You guessed it! White dudes.

AM I TRYING TO BRING THE WHITE MAN DOWN?

No. I am a white man. That wouldn't serve me well at all.

What I'm trying to do, and what feminism is trying to do, is bring the other genders up.

While an understandable response to this idea for men is a defensive one, considering so many of the bad things in history have been caused by men (by so many, I mean, like, all of them), that's also a positive response because it means you're accessing empathy.

You don't want to be seen as the "bad guy" (what a misandristic term!). You don't hate women. You've never oppressed women. Of course you haven't. Oppression doesn't happen on the individual level.

But it happens. And as a man, particularly one who is white (like me!), m are granted a lot of privileges that stem from hundreds of years of oppression. You get those privileges whether you choose to have them or not. The only choice you get is what you do with your privilege.

Do you use it to make for a more equitable society for people of all genders?

Or do you keep whining about how feminists hate men and distracting yourself and others from serious issues of inequality?

Your call, dudes.

Hi! I'm a feminist.

No, I don't hate men.

No, I don't think men are evil.

No, I don't think all men are rapists.

Yes, I want equity for all genders.

Yes, I'm a feminist.

SOCIAL

JUSTICE

COMPETENCE

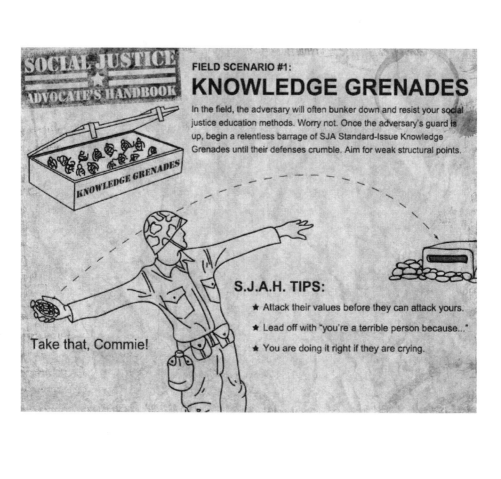

SOCIAL JUSTICE ADVOCATE'S HANDBOOK

KNOWLEDGE GRENADES

FIELD SCENARIO #1:

KNOWLEDGE GRENADES

In the field, the adversary will often bunker down and resist your social justice education methods. Worry not. Once the adversary's guard is up, begin a relentless barrage of SJA Standard-Issue Knowledge Grenades until their defenses crumble. Aim for weak structural points.

S.J.A.H. TIPS:

★ Attack their values before they can attack yours.

★ Lead off with "you're a terrible person because..."

★ You are doing it right if they are crying.

Take that, Commie!

CHAPTER 25

WHY MY APPROACH TO SOCIAL JUSTICE IS BETTER THAN YOURS

YOU HAVE YOUR WAY. I HAVE MY WAY. AS FOR THE RIGHT WAY, THE CORRECT WAY, AND THE ONLY WAY, IT DOES NOT EXIST.

—Friedrich Nietzsche

The way I approach social justice and ally work has a distinct flavor. Some would call it sweet, but I think it's a bit more spicy-sweet, like Thai food. I don't often do things in my life by accident, and in the case of how I do social justice work, it is extremely on purpose. My flavor is even so noticeable that having read this far in this book, you're likely taken aback by the title of this chapter. Well, that actually leads me into my first point.

I TRY NOT TO TALK DOWN TO PEOPLE

Did the title of this chapter irk you a bit? It likely did. That's a reasonable reaction. I wanted to make a point (and I'm sorry!).

How could I possibly know that my approach is better than yours? I don't know you. I don't know your experiences. Nor do I know your dispositions. I can't know my approach is better, so why would I start the conversation out that way? Unfortunately, a lot of folks I've seen trying to do good start things out this way.

You can't know what people know without asking them, so start by asking. Get a sense for what they know and attempt to build on that; don't just assume they have everything wrong and start at square one. At the very least, people likely have a decent idea of what is wrong with society, even if they don't know how to fix it.

An important thing to remember is that you weren't always an "expert" on the stuff you now know so much about. In fact, it's likely that you've only known something for a short amount of time. I'm learning and relearning things every day; it's a huge part of doing this work. Try to keep that in mind when you approach someone, because it'll help you keep yourself out of the ever-seductive ivory tower.

Icebreaker prompts to figure out on what level to start a conversation:

1. Tell me what you know about the hardships of X group.

2. When in your past have you felt like life was just plain unfair?

3. What's your experience with / knowledge of social justice and equality issues?

I TRY TO MEET PEOPLE WHERE THEY ARE

Following up on the first point, I'm drawing on a phrase I learned in grad school. In trying to help people learn and grow, it's wise to meet them where they are. That is, to use terms, concepts, and ideas they are familiar with to help them begin to grasp slightly more advanced concepts. Nobody should start out eating a sundae; they should get a sense of what banana and ice cream and strawberry and chocolate and peanuts taste like individually to know how much more delicious they are when you mash them all together. OK. Now I'm hungry.

The biggest issue here is that you might know 100 percent of an issue that your target knows (let's be generous) 10 percent. And you, being a well-intentioned person, want your target to instantly go from 10 percent to 100 percent. Well, sorry friend, but that's not how it works. Instead, try aiming for 11 percent. Or, if you really want to challenge them, 12 percent. Challenge is OK if there's not too much. Too much challenge and they'll snap like a dry waffle cone. Sorry.

I'm still in sundae mode.

I create all my graphics and writings with a particular knowledge level in mind. For most of what I do, that level is introductory. But in some, I build on introductory concepts and expand them into more complex ideas. That's because the goal of my work is to help "average" people help other people understand these issues; I'm not defending my dissertation on sexuality and gender (as some folks seem to think).

Tips for meeting people where they are:

1. Figure out where they are (see the first point above).

2. Be patient, and don't skip steps. People may fake understanding if you go too fast, and that doesn't help anyone.

3. Think about where you were when you first confronted these issues (not foolproof but a decent place to start).

I TRY NOT TO BE OVERBEARING OR AGGRAVATING

Looking back at the title of this chapter, you may have been a bit pissed off when you read it. If you're like a lot of folks, you may have started reading the chapter with the sole intention of finding something wrong that you could correct or denounce later—and all this happened before you even heard what I have to say. This happens in real-life conversations about social justice all too often.

Well-intentioned people see an opportunity to educate someone on a social justice issue (e.g., they overhear the person say something homophobic) and they pounce. Before the unsuspecting student (prey) knows what's happening, the social justice educator (predator) has ripped out their throat and is nibbling on their entrails. Yum.

Just bringing up a lot of these issues is enough to put someone on the defensive. People don't like being attacked. When they sense that happening, they'll prepare their defenses. Once someone is holed up in a bunker with you whipping knowledge grenades at them, it's guaranteed to be a long siege. (Once I wrote that last sentence, I couldn't resist drawing it, which resulted in the comic in this chapter, which led to the theme of this book—true story.) People don't often change their minds on important issues by force (read up on holy wars).

Ways to avoid a social justice holy war:

1. Use "I" statements whenever possible (e.g., "I use this term because" instead of "You should use this term because").

2. Dip your toes into the pool before you cannonball. It's not good to take a potential social justice trainee (victim) by surprise.

3. Know what your triggers are and how to navigate them (Check out "Navigating Triggers" by Kathy Obear for some help).

I CREATE CUTE GRAPHICS AND MAKE SILLY JOKES

Social issues could be lightly described as hot-button issues, meaning they are likely to make calm become nuclear if pushed too hard. It's important to be aware of this and attempt to mitigate it when you're chatting with people about this stuff. There are a number of ways one can do this; I use cute graphics, and in person, I use humor.

For me, humor is the best tool for diffusing a situation. I've been doing it since I was just a wee little social justice educator, and it's my go-to tool. In some situations, this doesn't work well, and there are definitely great (or better) alternatives. But I've learned that for my style of writing and talking, cute graphics and silly jokes work.

Figure out what works for you.

The big idea here is to create a space that feels safe and welcoming for anyone you're chatting with about social justice and equality issues. As you've learned above, there's plenty stacked up against it going well. Don't do something you're not comfortable with (e.g., trying to be funny if you're not or trying to be warm-hearted if you're naturally more room temp), and experiment to find what works. Just do something to make the space as safe and welcoming as you can.

Some ways to make a space feel a bit safer:

1. Respect/establish confidentiality. Ask if the person wants the talk to remain confidential, and if so, make it so.

2. If you share, they will share. This is one of the few real "rules" I can think of that always work.

3. Remind the person/group that you aren't perfect (because you aren't) and are still learning yourself (because you are).

I TRY TO KEEP TRYING AND TO KEEP LEARNING

I don't always do the things above well (or at all), but I always try to. And if one approach doesn't work for an issue, I try another. Trying and failing and trying again is a huge part of social justice work, and it's something I'm always doing. Knowing that I'm going to fail allows me to take the risks necessary to keep growing, instead of thinking that if I don't take risks, I may not fail. Because failing is inevitable. (Hammered in enough?)

If you're "educating" people in social justice or equality issues and it turns out they know something you don't, great! Ask questions; learn more; let them teach you. You'll be better off for it on your next adventure, and you'll have established a genuine trust with that group. Trying and failing often leads to learning. Let it. It's good for you, like aloe vera. Don't pretend you knew something you didn't. That's not good for you or the group, like tasting aloe vera. (Seriously, don't taste it; it's horrendous.)

And above all, try to keep trying. Achieving social justice is definitely possible, but it's not going to happen after one toss of a knowledge grenade. Keep hurling those things relentlessly! Wait. That might be bad. The point is not to give up. If you give up, the war is lost. Actually, let's try not to stop using the word "war."

What helps me to keep fighting this war:

1. I remind myself why I do what I do. Sometimes I do that in writing; sometimes it's through a quality convo with a friend.

2. I spend time with positive people and do my best to interact with others who have a similar cause.

3. I save the few encouraging e-mails I get for when things get rough.

CHAPTER 26

BEING WELL-INTENTIONED ISN'T GOOD ENOUGH

NO ONE WOULD REMEMBER THE GOOD SAMARITAN IF HE'D ONLY HAD GOOD INTENTIONS; HE HAD MONEY AS WELL.

—*Margaret Thatcher*

Throughout my career, I've created many resources intended to inform people on how they can use language to be more inclusive and respectful. A common reaction is "How can you regulate language? What's offensive to one person is not to another. What matters are your intentions."

My response is universally "Intentions don't matter; outcome matters."

I will elaborate on that more in a bit, but first I want to pose another question that I think is important for understanding all of this—and posit an answer.

WHY THE FASCINATION WITH INTENTIONS?

Why is it that we have such a high regard for intentions and try hard to be (and cherish) "well-intentioned" people? What is it about intentions that attracts us like mosquitos to a bug zapper? (You'll realize soon that this simile is even more apt than you might know.)

There are a couple of things at play here that lead to the focus on intentions rather than outcomes: the ideas of "political correctness" and "victim blaming" and, most importantly, how they interact. Before I can explain the interaction, let me explain what they are.

Victim Blaming 101

The phrase "blaming the victim," coined by psychologist William Ryan in his midseventies book about race and poverty, Blaming the Victim, is tossed around a lot these days surrounding instances of rape (and date rape). The concept hasn't changed much in the past forty years. So, what is it?

Victim blaming is when a perpetrator of some crime deflects the fault back onto the person they committed the crime against, effectively justifying the crime and absolving themselves of any guilt. As I mentioned before, the most common use of it these days is in cases involving rape, and the most common argument is "She was asking for it" (usually because of how she was dressed or because of a previous relationship with the offender).

Sound screwy to you? Then you're in the minority. Most people (in studies and polls) seem to think that rape victims are at least partially to blame for being raped. That says a lot about a lot, but tuck it away for a minute while we focus on the other part of this equation.

"Political Correctness"

I don't think anything about this book, my website, or even my live show is encouraging being "politically correct." I support being inclusive. I wrote an entire chapter about the difference between being inclusive and politically correct, so refer to that (Chapter 30) if you want to hear more on this particular subject. For this chapter, all that's important is knowing that a lot of people oppose what I do because they oppose the idea of being "PC."

The opposition to "political correctness" appears to be strong across the political spectrum. Regardless of left or right leanings, people don't like to be told what to say, and they don't like being censored. I echo those feelings. Hooray! Something we all can agree on.

The problem is how this gets twisted with victim blaming into some confusing and contradictory outcomes.

VICTIM BLAMING + POLITICAL CORRECTNESS = INTENTIONS > OUTCOMES

If math isn't your thing, the heading here means that victim blaming and political correctness interact in such a way as to lead folks to believe and support the idea that intentions are more important than outcomes. As I mentioned before, outcomes are what matter most (more on that in the next section; patience for now), so this is a problem. But how does it play out?

The Situation

Let's consider an example. A well-intentioned cisgender person (Friend A) calls his trans* friend (Friend B) a "hermaphrodite," because he's trying to use the most technical term he can think of and strays away from trans* because it's so close to "tranny" (all of this being an extremely common mode of thinking). Friend A is trying to be a good dude and a good friend. But Friend B corrects him, pointing out that "trans" is a better term, and "hermaphrodite" has negative, science-experiment, uncomfortable vibes.

The Reaction

Well-intentioned Friend A is now spurned because he feels that he was trying his best to be inclusive and that Friend B is just (a) nit-picking, (b) impossible to please, (c) asking too much, or (d) has a problem with cisgender people. He argues, either verbally with his friend or nonverbally with himself in his head, that he meant well, and his friend should recognize that.

We've all been there, Friend A. It's OK! You're surrounded by friends.

The Problem

People in general don't like to be told what to say—this goes for well-intentioned people as well as jerks. When our well-intentioned person went out of his way to say what he thought was the "right" thing, he was stretching himself in two ways: he was saying something he wasn't comfy with, but saying it because he thought it was "PC" (i.e., "right"), and he was taking a risk to try and be a good dude to Friend B at the expense of failing and feeling like a jerk. And when that failure happened, he jumped from the Political Correctness Frying Pan (patent pending) into the Victim Blaming Fire.

Being corrected by Friend B when Friend A already feels like he is being "corrected" by society at large (being "PC") is tough medicine to swallow. Throw in the fact that the reason he was being "PC" was due to empathetic concern for Friend A's feelings and wants—his intent was to make Friend A feel safer/comfier/faster/stronger (sorry, went Daft Punk there)—and you have a recipe for emotional confusion.

To protect himself from feeling like a bad person (he's not, mind you, but people are quick to take a correction for a particular behavior as code for "You're a bad person"), Friend A has to deflect blame to someone or something else. He can get pissed at society for wanting him to be "PC," but society is never an easy target for aggression, so instead he gets pissed at Friend B for being "impossible to please" and ignoring his good intentions. This is how victim blaming works. Making this seem like his friend's fault will allow him to feel better about himself—after all, his friend is the trans* one, who has to expect to be misunderstood or mislabeled. *Friend B is basically asking for it.*

WHY DO OUTCOMES MATTER MORE THAN INTENTIONS?

This is the real doozy. This is a fight I fight every day. "Why am I fighting a war against well-intentioned folks?" you might ask. Well, I'm not. I think well-intentioned folks are awesome. I identify as a well-intentioned folk. But I'm going to stick by my guns: intentions, in the grand scheme, don't mean squat.

When good intentions go bad

The first (and biggest) issue with intentions is how often good intentions go bad. A common reason they go bad is because we, as individuals, have individual wants and needs that are different from one another. How you manifest your good intentions and how I manifest mine are likely different, and how the object of our intentions receives them will likely be just as different. We often treat others how we want to be treated, instead of how they want to be treated. (We know what that's called, don't we?)

This pans out especially poorly any time there is a cultural divide.

What is good, nice, or helpful in one culture (family, workplace, city, region, country, continent) is not necessarily good, nice, or helpful in another. In fact, it might end up being just the opposite. Intentions are flawed.

But it's the thought that counts

Nope, actually, it's not. Even among close friends, arguments are often caused due to the slightest bit of misunderstanding. Why would you not expect this to happen with strangers?

Let's say I, as a well-intentioned Sam, bought a gift for my friend that I thought she would absolutely love (true story). Now let's say that, unbeknownst to me, this gift turned out to be something that triggered an incredibly visceral, damaging memory from her past. Should she wear this thing and tote it around because of how thoughtful I was, or should she tell me what happened and/or decline the gift?

She certainly felt pressured to do the former (because it was a gift, and beggars can't be choosers, and it's the thought that counts, and other clichés), but thankfully for her emotional and psychological well-being, and our friendship, she did the latter. (End of story.)

Intentions are capricious and theoretical

In any relationship (between two individuals, a teacher and a class, one group and another) countless interactions will take place, all bearing an immeasurable weight of intentions. Those intentions are bound to change from interaction to interaction and be interpreted (or misinterpreted) based on the receiver's mood or disposition.

What's more troublesome is that intentions are theoretical agreements made between the intender and the intendee, without the intendee's awareness of the agreement or the terms. You wouldn't mentally sell someone a car, mentally draw up all the paperwork, and mentally collect the money, and then, after presenting this deal to the person in real life and in past tense (i.e., "You just bought this car from me, bro. Where my dollas at?"), snap when they aren't OK with the "deal" they just made, would you? No. You wouldn't.

Following that example, it is unreasonable for us to hold fast to our intentions after they backfire. The people you are interacting with don't necessarily know your intentions, nor should they trump how your actions made them feel—and if they are offended or hurt by whatever well-intentioned thing you just said, they are in the worst possible mind-set to be buying a car.

Outcomes are consistent and real

On an individual level, outcomes are relatively consistent and predictable. If someone says X to me, I'll likely respond Y. Or, more refined, if someone says X to me, and I'm feeling Z, I'll likely respond Y. For example, if someone calls me a "fag," and I'm in a good mood, I'll respond Socratically by asking them questions and helping them get to their own conclusion of why they shouldn't be calling me that word. It doesn't matter if they said it as a joke, didn't mean anything by it, or said it "because you're wearin' them there flip-flops, boy." (The guy who told me that after a comedy show was a keeper.)

What's more important is that outcomes happen externally. It doesn't matter if you didn't intend to hit that bunny with your car, you did. You were a well-intentioned driver, and now you have a dead bunny. What are you going to do about it? You can try to adjust your driving for the future (pay more attention, drive slower, eat fewer burritos, etc.), or you can blame the bunny for its furry doom (shouldn't've been there; it was asking for it). In either case, it happened, regardless of your intentions, and now you get to choose how to move on.

MOVING BEYOND GOOD INTENTIONS

When people ask me what I do for a living, I like to respond that I help good people be better people. Well-intentioned people are good people. We all just always have a little ways to go to be better people, and it all takes place after the outcome, not before it.

Don't take it personally

It was not my intention to break a personal record for as many clichés as possible in one chapter, so whoops. But seriously: if you're a well-intentioned person and your good intentions backfire, don't take it personally. It happens. The outcome may have been bad, but that doesn't mean *you* are.

There's a difference there. We are the sum total of our experiences; we aren't defined by one mistake. It's easy to think that, to fall into that trap, but as soon as you take it personally when someone doesn't react well to your good intentions, things are only going to get worse—and you'll soon have a whole colony of dead bunnies on your hands.

Also, is "colony" not one of the cutest animal plurals you've ever heard? Bunnies really do it for me, so please, for the sake of my psyche, stop killing them.

Learn from your mistakes

You probably think I mean, in a follow-up to the last point, you should try to avoid whatever created that outcome to not have it happen again, right? Wrong.

Focus less on your intentions, the other people, and what happened and more on yourself. If you don't take it personally when you screw up, you'll have a better chance at remedying a situation. If you don't get frustrated when you are trying to be inclusive and aren't sure of the best word to say, you'll do a much better job at being inclusive and saying the "right" things.

Remember, the same action with the same intention can result in an infinite number of outcomes. The only constant is you and how you react to the other person's reaction, regardless of how it goes. Learn what your triggers are, learn how you can lessen them, and don't allow yourself to continue tripping over the same roots.

Open yourself up to failure-learning

It's funny to me how much flak I get about this intentions thing. People harp on me about how intentions should matter more—"Everyone doesn't know exactly what to say all the time like [I] do," etcetera—when it often feels like a majority of my time each day goes to cleaning dead bunnies off my car (metaphorical dead bunnies off my metaphorical car—I'm not an actual bunny-slayer. Remember, I love bunnies. And I ride a bicycle.).

I'm a well-intentioned person, and everything I do professionally is a manifestation of those good intentions, but the outcomes are often bad. But I'm here to fail/learn, and I've learned how to fail/learn more gracefully every day. I am a good person who is trying to be a better person. To be frank, this book and everything I write wouldn't be nearly the quality it is if it weren't for the amazing readership I've cultivated that doesn't hesitate to correct me when I fail, over and over and over and…OK. Enough.

Realizing that you're likely going to fail and being OK with that is what helps make failing and learning unite to become failure-learning. The two ideas have so blurred into one for me that only a little hyphen separates them. You're going to screw up. Count on it. I'm going to go out on a limb and use another (yes, another) cliché here and remind you that everybody falls down, but it's what you do when you get back up that matters.

Different intentions.

Same oily outcome.

CHAPTER 27

NO SUCH THING AS A POSITIVE STEREOTYPE

"DO YOU DRINK?" "OF COURSE, I JUST SAID I WAS A WRITER."

—*Stephen King*

As a reminder, positive stereotypes are assumptions about an entire group or identity (e.g., gay men) that are considered to be "good." Some examples of positive stereotypes of gay men, for example: artsy, friendly, fun, social, well-spoken, well-dressed, well-groomed, fit. The list goes on. Those are all good things, yeah? There can't be any harm in perpetuating those stereotypes, right?

Wrong.

DRILL: See how many positive gender-related stereotypes you can come up with in five minutes. Write like the wind, don't overthink it or second guess yourself, and think about the list you came up with as you read the rest of this chapter.

Positive stereotypes exist for just about every identity and have the capacity to be just as damaging as the negative ones. You don't think so? Well read on, and let's see if I can change your mind.

POSITIVE STEREOTYPES SET THE BAR UNREALISTICALLY HIGH

Have you ever met a gay guy who wasn't fit? Or a black guy who wasn't good at sports? Or a woman who wasn't caring? I'm going to guess you have. Now, the important part: did you realize that you were slightly disappointed or perturbed when you found out about the lack of those traits? I'm going to guess you didn't realize it, but you probably were.

Let's take the list of positive stereotypes I wrote above about gay men: artsy, friendly, fun, social, well-spoken, well-dressed, well-groomed, fit. That's a pretty tall order for anyone to fill, and the list goes on and on. And that's just focusing on where the "gay" and "man" identities intersect. "Gay" comes with a whole different set of unique stereotypes, and so does "man," all of which these gay men "should" embody.

Thanks to socialized positive stereotypes, every gay man you meet is being evaluated by a ridiculously tough rubric. If he falls short (let's say he's a bit chubby, or antisocial), he's going to disappoint you. Who wants a *B-* gay friend when there are so many *A+* gay men out there? (There aren't, actually, at least not based on the fulfillment of all positive stereotypes.)

Lesson learned: don't be disappointed when your gay friend isn't helpful in picking out a cute outfit the next time you go shopping. (You can call me. I'm not gay, but I'm great at putting together outfits.)

POSITIVE STEREOTYPES CAN INHIBIT AN INDIVIDUAL'S ABILITY TO PERFORM

You've heard that Asian people are good at math, right? Well, tell an Asian person that right before a math exam and you increase their potential…to bomb it.

Research has shown that perceived positive stereotypes, when brought into the forefront of an individual's mind, can actually make them do worse at the thing they are supposed to be able to do better. In a recent study by Cheryan & Bodenhausen, the researchers made Asian American women explicitly aware of their ethnicity (and the social expectations attached to it) right before testing their math skills and saw that they were more likely to collapse under the pressure and do poorly on the test.

This is fascinating because it is a quantifiable way of measuring what has been described as a crippling social pressure caused by positive stereotypes. But it's also depressing, because, well, did you read the last paragraph? Read it again. That's why.

Lesson learned: if you find yourself in the Cash Cab and a math question comes up, "Dude, you're Asian. Of course you know the answer" might not be the most effective pep talk. (But tag me in. Six words: Math Bowl, eighth grade, first place.)

POSITIVE STEREOTYPES ARE ALIENATING AND DEPRESSING TO INDIVIDUALS WHO ARE SUPPOSED TO POSSESS THEM BUT DON'T

Being a member of a targeted or minority group is potentially alienating, particularly if you're often surrounded by people who don't identify that way. You will often feel alone, not good enough, or looked down upon. This is likely not news to you.

But all of those negative feelings are amplified if you don't even feel like you can connect with your target or minority group membership because you don't live up to the hype. That is, if you already feel like you're alone because you're the only person of your identity in a social setting, you're going to feel even more alone if you don't even feel like you fit in with yourself (or how you imagine you're supposed to be).

I have an example a friend shared with me. Following is his story:

I'm a black man who grew up surrounded by white people. Growing up, I was the only black person in my neighborhood, my school, and sometimes it felt like the entire town. I never played basketball. I can't rap or dance well—I don't even like hip hop. I'm really good at video games, and I watch baseball. When I got to college, my skin made me too black to fit in with the white kids, and my skills/hobbies weren't black enough to fit in with the black kids.

This can be applied to just about any group membership that carries with it positive stereotypes (and, as I mentioned before, just about all of them do). It sucks to feel like you're in the minority sometimes. It sucks even more to feel like you're not even good enough for the minority, feeling individually marginalized within an already marginalized group.

Lesson learned: befriend people because of who they are as people, not the traits you assume will come with their group memberships. That is, don't try and make friends with a black guy because you need a point guard for your rec league team. (Also, don't call me, unless you want someone to bring orange slices for halftime. Then I'm your guy 'cuz I cut a mean orange slice!)

DRILL: Ever been the "victim" of a positive stereotype? Tell your story of that experience, or share your reactions to times this has happened, to a friend who shares the identity that stereotype was based on. See if their experience has been similar or different. Now do the same with someone who doesn't have that identity. Go, go, go!

SO, WHAT DO WE DO?

I've noticed that we, as a society, have gotten to the point where, in most cases, people aren't flinging around negative stereotypes that often—unless you're hanging out with some good-ol'-fashioned racists. Modern racism is much more subtle.

Most people nowadays have no problem casually tossing around positive stereotypes. Even many of the people who are up for leading the fight against prejudice seem to be completely OK with reinforcing positive stereotypes, because, as I said before, "What's the harm?" Well, now you know.

Positive stereotypes are just as dangerous as negative stereotypes. One could argue (as I would) that they are more dangerous, because of how we generally don't think of them as dangerous. They are like cats that are really pissed off all the time for no reason. You look at them and they seem cuddly, so you want to pick them up and hug them. Then bam! Claw City is settled on your forearm and population growth is booming!

The next time you're hanging with a friend and they say, "Gay men are so fashionable" (heard it twice the week I wrote this, once from a gay man), or anything of the like, let them know that type of belief can be just as damaging as "Gay men are so child molesty" (only heard this once in my life, thankfully). If you don't feel up to that challenge, give them a copy of this book (passive aggressiveness is a trait that crosses all identity lines and group memberships).

And hey—free book!

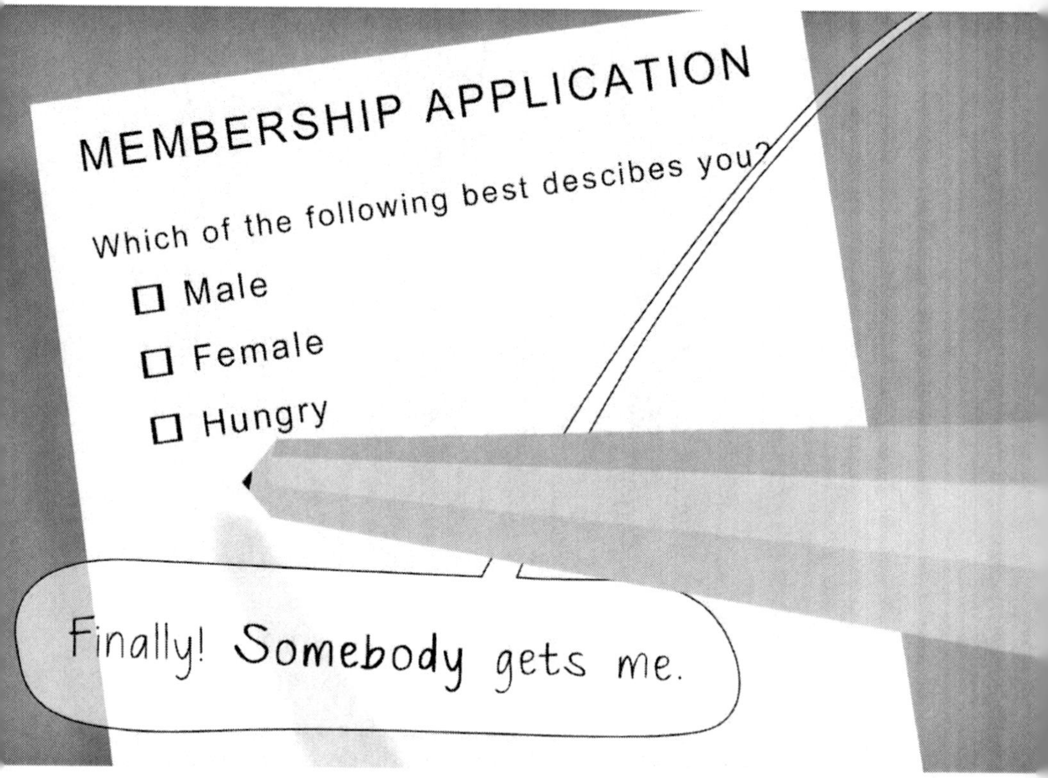
MEMBERSHIP APPLICATION
Which of the following best descibes you?
Male
Female
Hungry
Finally! Somebody gets me.

CHAPTER 28

MAKING FORMS GENDER INCLUSIVE

MAYBE IT'S WRONG-FOOTED TRYING TO FIT PEOPLE INTO THE WORLD, RATHER THAN TRYING TO MAKE THE WORLD A BETTER PLACE FOR PEOPLE.

—*Paul McHugh*

A lot of people are unsure of how to make an inclusive gender or sex question on a form and default to "Are you male or female?" Let's not do that. Read on for some best practices and suggestions to make your forms more gender inclusive.

The first question I would ask in response to this dilemma is "What relevance does gender have to your membership application process?" I've often found that the reason people ask for gender is simply because they always have. Is gender truly a relevant and necessary factor in making your selections (or whatever you're doing with your applications)? In a lot of cases it's irrelevant. If it's irrelevant, don't ask. Problem solved. If you think you need to ask it, let's discuss the implications.

Let's assume you've thought through that first question and want to proceed with a gender question on your application.

SAMPLE OPTIONS / FOODS FOR THOUGHT

Super simple solution, but one that is not easily sortable (in a spreadsheet):

1. I identify my gender as...

_____ (fill in the blank)

If you don't need gender, but would prefer to have it, here is one way you could do it:

2. I identify my gender as...

[] Man

[] Woman

[] Trans*

[] _____ (fill in the blank)

[] Prefer not to disclose

If you absolutely need to know gender, my next easy suggestion would be to simply remove the "not disclose" option:

3. I identify my gender as...

[] Man

[] Woman

[] Trans*

[] _____ (fill in the blank)

If you'd rather not have a fill in the blank because it will complicate things (e.g., make it harder to sort a spreadsheet), but you want to be incredibly inclusive and specific, here's another suggestion:

4. I identify my gender as...

[] Man

[] Woman

[] Transgender

[] Transsexual

[] Genderqueer

[] Nongendered

[] Agender
[] Genderless
[] Non-binary
[] Trans Man
[] Trans Woman
[] Third-Gender
[] Two-Spirit
[] Bigender
[] Genderfluid
[] Transvestite

And if you'd rather have fewer options, even at the expense of inclusivity/specificity:

5. I identify my gender as…
[] Man
[] Woman
[] Trans*

And finally, if you need to know sex rather than gender (the only examples that pop into my mind for a reason why are medical), here's a way you can do it and still be inclusive:

6. I identify my sex as…
[] Female
[] Male
[] Intersex
[] MtF Female
[] FtM Male

A FEW EXPLANATIONS AND CONSIDERATIONS FOR THESE EXAMPLES

One of the things you'll notice as a common thread throughout all of the questions is the prompt "I identify my…" I recommend this because it begins the action as a form of empowerment, instead of other options I've seen that often take the power to decide away from the individual answering the question.

Also, consider how you are going to be using the data you're collecting before you decide how to collect it. If you're planning on matching people up based on gender (e.g., partners for activities, team relationships), you might ask for the applicants to report their gender but also ask them which gender they would feel most comfortable working with. Then you can use their responses to place them in self-described comfortable partnerships, or choose to challenge them if you would rather see them working outside of their comfort zone.

I'm not a big fan of exhaustive lists when trying to describe identities (see #4) because they are rarely exhaustive. And if you miss one or two, but include fifteen others, those one or two get the sense of super-marginalization. This feeling of super-marginalization gets heavier with each additional identity you add, because you're making it more and more clear that you tried your hardest to include everyone, so you may not think the identity you left out is worth including.

LET'S EXTRAPOLATE THIS

Of all the chapters in this book, this is likely one of the most concrete. It's helpful in that way, but it can also be limiting. I want to take a moment to explain why I wrote this "how-to" type chapter and to discuss the implications for future considerations, with hope that you will be able to apply what we've done here to future endeavors that may not be directly related to gender questions on applications.

Why did I write it?

This chapter was the result of an e-mail. Someone wrote me and asked, quite frankly, how to do this properly. I replied to the e-mail by posting an article on my site containing most of what you read above.

Since posting it on my site, it has been one of the top visited articles as a result of Google searches. Searches like "how do I make applications gender neutral?" "ways to be inclusive on application forms," or "male/female question on applications what's a better question?" (which, itself, is a pretty terrible way to ask a question) all end up directing people to the article on my site thousands of times a month.

This is incredibly encouraging to me because it represents a shift in culture. I grew up in an extremely checkboxy world. You were male or female; White, Black, Hispanic, Asian, or other. Organizations seem to be making a shift toward removing the stigma of being other.

I couldn't be happier.

What does this mean for the future version of yourself?

What I'm gleaning from all this is that now is a time when rabble-rousing is far less dangerous than it was just ten years ago. You can now speak up if you are a member of an organization (workplace, school, etc.) that is being gender exclusive (e.g., no gender-neutral restrooms, no protection for gender identity in hiring/firing, or, obviously, the "male or female?" question on any forms), and hopefully do so without risking your job.

So speak up. Use this chapter as the starting point for an ongoing discussion in ways you can make your workplace more inclusive of people of all genders and identities.

Are the people making important decisions for the entire organization all of one gender? Change that. It will make the organization stronger, allowing you to better serve your membership and relate to the external community as a whole.

Are you making it clear that your organization is inclusive of people of all gender identities by holding trainings and instituting gender-inclusive policies and procedures? Make sure you are. It will make for a safer space for everyone and will make your organization more attractive to folks who are trans* or genderqueer.

Can you honestly say that you would feel comfortable doing what you're doing and being a member of your organization, no matter what identities comprised you?

Don't stop rabble-rousing until you can.

CHAPTER 29

ADOPTING THE TERM PARTNER
(AND USING OTHER INCLUSIVE LANGUAGE)

IT IS ONLY HUMAN SUPREMACY, WHICH IS AS UNACCEPTABLE AS RACISM AND SEXISM, THAT MAKES US AFRAID OF BEING MORE INCLUSIVE.

—*Ingrid Newkirk*

Using the term "partner" to replace boyfriend or girlfriend is widely suggested as a means to speak more inclusively, allowing gay, lesbian, or bisexual people to feel more comfortable around you.

When I use this term to refer to my partner around straight people, it often results in raised eyebrows, and sometimes discomfort. I'm regularly asked, "Why did you say your partner instead of your girlfriend?" What's the point? Let me explain the three main reasons why I have replaced boyfriend/girlfriend/husband/wife with partner.

IT DOESN'T HURT ANYONE TO SAY PARTNER

Using the term "partner," particularly when inquiring about a stranger's partner ("How long have you been with your partner?" instead of "How long have you been with your girlfriend?"), avoids the heteronormative assumption that the guy you are asking has a girlfriend/wife or the gal you are asking has a boyfriend/husband.

If a person is straight, there is generally no harm done. A straight man may raise an eyebrow at the term partner instead of hearing you ask about his girlfriend, but that's usually it. A really homophobic straight man may get offended at the thought he might be gay, but that's another issue for another book. (Short version: research says the more homophobic someone is, the more likely they are struggling internally with their sexuality—whoops.)

On the other hand, if a guy is queer and you ask, "Do you have a girlfriend?" you're doing a really good job of making him feel marginalized. And marginalizing people is rarely good. I say rarely because of course there are situations where everything is appropriate, but that's another issue for another book. (Short version: a historical example of a group I would argue would have been appropriate to marginalize would be the National Socialist political party in the early twentieth century) Look at me, giving away book ideas like they're flapjacks.

SAYING PARTNER MAKES QUEER PEOPLE FEEL SAFER AROUND ME

Taking the initiative to use an inclusive word like partner is tantamount to pinning a button to my chest that says "I care." This goes for everyone: straight, bi-, gay, lesbian, or otherwise. Partner is a recognized word of safety and concern within the queer community.

One of the toughest things about identifying with a targeted group is knowing who you can confide in and who you might want to avoid, at least until the times change a bit. Language is an effective way to inform others, particularly people who don't know you very well, that you fall into the former group, the group that can be trusted.

It's a really simple, non-burdensome way to make a substantial, palpable shift in welcomitude (not a word, but you get it; don't be a jerk) of the communities you relate with. That alone should be enough, but there's more!

USING PARTNER REMINDS FOLKS WE STILL HAVE PROGRESS TO MAKE

Many people get comfortable in their lives and become more and more oblivious to the simple fact that we do not live in an equitable society where people of all identities have the same access to resources. Inclusive language is a great direct step to creating a safe space for everyone, but it also has a powerful indirect effect.

Intentionally using inclusive language, like saying partner instead of boyfriend or girlfriend, will often create an opportunity for a discussion about why you use such language. As I mentioned before, this happens to me quite often. When a question like this is asked, an educational opportunity is presented, and it's the best opportunity of all because it stems from genuine curiosity.

A lot of folks think social justice should be left to "social justice people," the same way they think we should leave whatever type of work they do to them and other people who do whatever their job is. What they don't realize is that most "social justice people" are generally "other type of work people" first and foremost who happen to have a passion for promoting social justice. They are generally people who, perhaps like yourself, weren't always aware of these issues, but as they learned more they became more curious, which made them learn more, which made them more curious, which made them…I think my keyboard is broken.

Inspiring curiosity is a great way to turn people who consider themselves "other type of work people" into "social justice people," one issue or topic at a time, until slowly it takes over their entire body like a warm and fuzzy cancer.

So when someone asks you, "Why do you say 'partner' instead of boyfriend or girlfriend?" you can respond, "You take the blue pill, the story ends; you wake up in your bed and believe whatever you want to believe. You take the red pill, you stay in Wonderland, and I show you how deep the rabbit hole goes."

WHY AM I ALWAYS TRYING TO USE THE MOST INCLUSIVE LANGUAGE I CAN

(…and, therefore, constantly learning what different groups consider inclusive?)

I just told you why. Every time I said "partner" in this chapter, you can exchange it for [choose an inclusive term], and every time I said "queer community," you can exchange it for [target group that identifies with that inclusive term].

I screw up a lot, and language is always shifting, but it's important to me that I do my best to find how people want me to describe them and to describe them properly, because, you know, all that stuff I said up there.

Being Inclusive

Political Correctness

CHAPTER 30

POLITICAL CORRECTNESS VS. BEING INCLUSIVE

THE GREATEST ENEMY OF CLEAR LANGUAGE IS INSINCERITY.

—*George Orwell*

I would never ask you to be politically correct. I get a lot of flak for some of my graphics and writing because people feel that I'm soap-boxing for political correctness, when that couldn't be further from the truth. Before you send me an e-mail, tweet, or Facebook message saying, "Sorry if I'm not all 'PC'...," know this: I've never asked you to be politically correct.

I ask you to be inclusive.

YES, THERE'S A DIFFERENCE

Before you get all hot and bothered, I want you to acknowledge the idea that there may be a significant difference between being politically correct and being inclusive. If you can't acknowledge this, there's no point in reading on. Head outside, de-stress, yell obscenities at strangers, then come back when you're ready.

Ready? OK...go.

What's the difference?

Political correctness is externally driven; being inclusive is internally driven. When people do something they consider to be "polit-ically correct" (using certain terms, acknowledging certain groups, etc.), it often conflicts with their values—they are doing it because they have been told they should, even if they don't believe it them-selves. In contrast, when people do things they consider to be "in-clusive," even if these things are the same as the politically correct things, they never conflict with their values because being inclusive is a value.

The Skinny on Political Correctness and Being Inclusive

Being politically correct is behaving in a way that will gain you approval from others. It makes you look good to those in power (vot-ers, friends, parents, teachers, Mark Zuckerberg) so that they will think favorably of you. It is externally driven, which means it is guid-ed by your understanding of what you think you should do to be viewed positively by others. Often times, political correctness com-promises one's values for "free speech" and equates to censorship, where a person chooses not to say something solely because they've been told not to.

Being inclusive is all about being a better person to other people. It is internally driven by your design to do what is right, or what will result in you showing the most respect you can for the people around you or in your life. Being inclusive is a mind-set. Once you have it in your mind that you want to make others feel more com-fortable around you, you'll find that you'll be looking for ways to do so. It's not about compromising your values; it's about refining and developing values of empathy and concern for the other. You won't feel uncomfortable censoring yourself from calling something "re-tarded"; in fact, you'll feel uncomfortable when you hear others do so.

LIMITATIONS (YES, THERE ARE ALWAYS THESE)

As with every good rule, there are exceptions, and I want to write about a few of those here before I get more sassy e-mails. Actually, scratch that—I love sassy e-mails. Send them my way even after you read this. But for now, let me address a few of the hangups that folks who are new to this "being inclusive" thing often get hung up on. In the grand scheme, they're more hiccups than hangups.

You don't have to be inclusive of everybody

"But Sam, what if someone believes that all people of XYZ group should be exterminated. Should I support that person's belief?"

Depends on which group they are talking about (kidding). No. You obviously should not support that belief. But seriously, it depends on who they are talking about (kidding again).

(Kinda.)

There is no absolute "right" or "wrong"

"I was saying Native American, but then someone who is Native American said she prefers the term American Indian. I told her she was wrong. She should know better."

Unfortunately, as with most aspects of life, this is one of those gray rather than black and white things. Rely on an internal compass guided by empathy and you'll be off to a good start, and when in doubt, follow the Platinum Rule.

Nobody's perfect: we're all learning

"I accidentally told my friend that soccer is gay, and then when I realized I said it, I yelled, 'I need to stop saying gay. Why am I so retarded?' so whoops. What now? I'm going to hell, aren't I?"

A professor/mentor of mine once told me it's inevitable that she'll act with hypocrisy, so she sets a goal to only do five hypocritical things each day. I believe similarly.

DON'T eat their faces off!

If they seemed well-intentioned, or even if you're not sure what their intent was, you'll attract more bees with honey than you will by being a jerk. You want more bees, don't you? Also, bees, here, means social justice friends.

fyi I was using that expression way before people were literally doing it.

...[non-inclusive word]...

Did you seriously just say that? I thought we were friends, but I can tell you that I am absolutely not friends with people who blindly hate an entire group of people, you blind group hater! People die because of language like that. You might as well kill them yourself. Is that what you want? Do you want to kill people, people killer? Oh, I bet that's exactly what you want you blind group hating people killer person who I thought was once maybe my friend but is certainly NOT! not anymore I'll tell you what.

CHAPTER 31

RESPONDING TO NON-INCLUSIVE LANGUAGE

ANGER IS THE ENEMY OF NON-VIOLENCE AND PRIDE IS A MONSTER THAT SWALLOWS IT UP.

—*Mahatma Gandhi*

Recognizing bigoted language is one thing; being prepared to respond when someone uses it is another altogether. Moving from being a conscious person to a social justice advocate is a shift from mindset to action.

There, as you could likely guess, good and bad approaches to social justice interventions. In this chapter, we are going to focus on some of the most common of both. Let's do it!

DON'T EAT THEIR FACES OFF

It's natural to be angry when you hear someone say a bigoted word, but being angry isn't going to help anything.

Even in "this day and age," there's a decent chance that the offending person doesn't even realize they are offending. This is something that might come as a shock, particularly if you're a socially conscious person, but trust me. True story: I have conversations with folks on a near-daily basis about how "nigger" is a *bad word*. Yes, true story.

Now, not everyone who uses bigoted language is going to be in the "doesn't realize they are doing something bad" category. There are a few other common categories: people who think words don't hurt and they should be able to say what they want (I call them "sticks and stoners"); people who use bigoted language because they equate it to other swearing or edginess ("not a big dealers"); and, of course, people whose bigoted language reflects their bigoted mind-set or perspective ("bigots"). There are others, I'm sure. But I digress.

In all four instances, being angry will only make the situation worse. If someone doesn't know what they were doing and you get mad at them, it's like yelling at an infant for spilling their formula (something that—and it pains me to say this—actually happens). If they don't think bigoted language is *really* that bad, your anger will only add to their impression that you're being melodramatic. And if the person is a big ol' bigot, trying to eat their face off might result in a dangerous situation for you.

What I'm trying to say is anger leads to hate, hate leads to suffering, and we don't want to lead anyone to the dark side.

DO KINDLY POINT OUT THEIR ERROR

The first step in responding to a person using non-inclusive language is addressing to the person that the language they are using isn't inslusive. This is an extremely important step, and one folks often skip over, but it's helpful because it sets the stage for how we will continue our response with all four of our bigoted language peeps from the first section.

This can play out in a number of ways. I'm a big fan of the Socratic Method, where you use questions to help the person come to a conclusion on their own. For example, if someone calls a transgender person a "hermaphrodite" I might ask, "Why'd you use that term?" That gives me a sense of what type of bigoted language user they might be. In the case of "hermaphrodite," it's often the case that people don't realize it's a non-inclusive term at all. I will then explain the history of the term hermaphrodite, addressing why it's considered to be such a negative word by many people, and ask them "Do you think it's a term that would make a trans* person in your life comfortable if you used it?"

But you can also do this more directly. If someone says "hermaphrodite" you can simply address it by replying, "Hey, not sure if you know this or not—most people don't—but hermaphrodite is considered to be a stigmatizing term."

Whatever your approach to address that the term someone is using is bigoted, the one thing I strongly recommend is doing it with as much kindness as you can muster.

DON'T MAKE THEM FEEL LIKE BAD PEOPLE

Focus on the behavior, not the behaver—or, to use real words, the actions, not the actor. It's really easy to inadvertently lump the two together, and people will be inclined to feel that you are.

There is a big difference between saying "Hey, this one thing you're doing is bad" and "Hey, you're a bad person." The first one is something that gives a person options, sets the scope of the problem in a surmountable way, and provides them with a clear path if they want to improve. The second one is just mean. Be intentional to show that you are not attacking them personally.

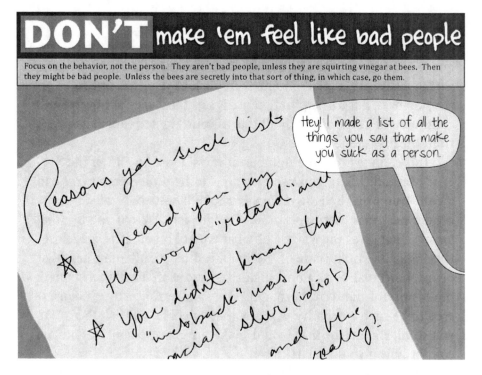

DON'T make 'em feel like bad people

Focus on the behavior, not the person. They aren't bad people, unless they are squirting vinegar at bees. Then they might be bad people. Unless the bees are secretly into that sort of thing, in which case, go them.

DO PROVIDE THEM WITH A CORRECTION FOR THE FUTURE

Following up on our "hermaphrodite" example from earlier, beyond simply addressing that the language a person is using is non-inclusive, you should try to provide them with alternatives for the future.

In the case of "hermaphrodite" you might explain to someone that a more inclusive term for someone with both female and male sex characteristiscs would be "intersex." Or perhaps they are using "hermaphrodite as a term for someone who is transgender (fairly common), so you might suggest they say "transgender person" or "trans person" if that's what they mean.

Further, it's helpful to explain the "why" behind the new term, in addition to giving it to them. "Intersex is better because it is a broad and inclusive term, and doesn't specifically reference any particular set of sex characteristics. 'Hermaphrodite,' on the other hand, describes someone who is 100% male and female, a biological impossibility in humans." And if they were referring to a transgender person, explain that "hermaphrodite" is a label that reflects a person's sex, not their gender.

DON'T REFLECT THEIR BEHAVIOR BACK

This probably sounds childish. *I know you are but what am I!* But it's a common coping mechanism for people when they are put into these bigoted-language-using situations and they aren't quite prepared for it. It commonly starts with the famous phrase "How would you like it if I called you..."

The problem with reflecting behavior back and starting that line of thought is our goal is to change behavior, not reinforce what's currently happening. We are trying to introduce a new way of thinking for someone, or at least help them see a situation from a different angle.

A good rule to go by is if any of your social justice oriented conversations start to sound like something two toddlers might be yelling at each other in a sandbox, get out of the sandbox.

great things to try to remember to say when someone says something that is inclusive. Other than the last one—that's just a courteous lie.

Social justice people often get a bad wrap as being too complainy and not enough congratulatey. I agree that this is often the case, and a lot of good would be done if we did a better job being congratulatey. Encouraging positive behavior can be just as (and more) effective in moving us toward progress as discouraging negative behavior.

Catch people doing something right. It'll make them feel warm and gooey inside, and it will also make it easier for the to swallow the next time you catch them doing something that could use a bit of improvement. They will realize you aren't a jerk who likes telling people what to do, but that you're a genuinely motivated social justice superfan and you want the world to be a better place.

You can do this in the moment or you can do it retroactively, by way of my second favorite cookie (ousted by the Genderbread Person, obviously): the Compliment Sandwich.

The Compliment Sandwich is like an Oreo, but instead of cream you have a corrective behavior and instead of two cookies you have affirmations of positive behavior they've done in the past. Start with a cookie ("I appreciate how you're saying "transgender" instead of "transgendered"), then cream 'em ("But it's also generally more inclusive to think of "transgender" as an adjective, not a noun—so "he's a transgender person" not "he's a transgender"), then round it out with another cookie ("And I think it's great that you've been so inquisitive about these things, and that you're looking to learn.")

APPENDIX

A. GLOSSARY

B. TRANS* ASTERISK

C. RECOMMENDED READING

D. HEARTFELT THANKS

APPENDIX A

GLOSSARY

I'M VERY SENSITIVE TO THE ENGLISH LANGUAGE. I STUDIED THE DICTIONARY OBSESSIVELY WHEN I WAS A KID AND COLLECT OLD DICTIONARIES. WORDS, I THINK, ARE VERY POWERFUL AND THEY CONVEY AN INTENTION.

—*Drew Barrymore*

Advocate – (noun) (1) a person who actively works to end intolerance, educate others, and support social equity for a marginalized group. (verb) (2) to actively support/plea in favor of a particular cause, the action of working to end intolerance, educate others, etc.

Agender - (noun) a person with no (or very little) connection to the traditional system of gender, no personal alignment with the concepts of either "man" or "woman," and see themselves as existing without gender (sometimes called Gender Neutrois, gender neutral, or genderless).

Ally(ship) – (noun) a straight identified person who supports, and respects for members of the LGBTQ community.

- While the word doesn't necessitate action, we consider people to be active allies who take action upon this support and respect, this also indicates to others that you are an ally.

- "Coming out" as an ally is when you reveal (or take an action that reveals) your support of the LGBTQ community. Because being an active supporter can, at times, be stigmatized and is not assumed many allies go through a "coming out process" in relation to being an ally.

Androgyny/ous – (adj) (1) a gender expression that has elements of both masculinity and femininity; (2) occasionally used in place of "intersex" to describe a person with both female and male anatomy.

Androsexual/Androphilic – (adj) attraction to men, males, and/or masculinity.

Aromantic - (adj) is a person who experiences little or no romantic attraction to others and/or a lack of interest in forming romantic relationships.

Asexual – (adj) having a lack of (or low level of) sexual attraction to others and/or a lack of interest or desire for sex or sexual partners.

- Asexuality exists on a spectrum from people who experience no sexual attraction or have any desire for sex to those who experience low levels and only after significant amounts of time, many of these different places on the spectrum have their own identity labels.

- Asexuality is different than celibacy in that it is a sexual orientation whereas celibacy is an abstaining from a certain action.

- Not all asexual people are aromantic.

Bigender – (adj) a person who fluctuates between traditionally "woman" and "man" gender-based behavior and identities, identifying with both genders (and sometimes a third gender).

Bicurious – (adj) a curiosity about having attraction to people of the same gender/sex (similar to questioning).

Biological Sex – (noun) a medical term used to refer to the chromosomal, hormonal and anatomical characteristics that are used to classify an individual as female or male or intersex. Often abbreviated to simply "sex".

- Often seen as simply a binary but as their are many combinations of chromosomes, horomones, and primary/secondary sex characteristics, it's more accurate to view this as a spectrum (which is also more inclusive of intersex people as well as trans*-identified people)

- Is commonly conflated with gender.

Biphobia – (noun) a range of negative attitudes (e.g., fear, anger, intolerance, resentment, or discomfort) that one may have/express towards bisexual individuals. Biphobia can come from and be seen within the queer community as well as straight society. **Biphobic** (adj) a word used to describe an individual who harbors some elements of this range of negative attitudes towards bisexual people.

- Really important to recognize that many of our "stereotypes" of bisexual people - they're overly sexual, greedy, it's just a phase - are negative and stigmatizing (and therefore biphobic) and that gay, straight, and many other queer individuals harbor these beliefs.

Bisexual – (adj) a person emotionally, physically, and/or sexually attracted to males/men and females/ women. This attraction does not have to be equally split between genders and there may be a preference for one gender over others.

- Can simply be shortened to "bi."
- Because it is the most commonly understood term outside of gay/straight many people who do not believe in the binary categories that bisexual can imply still use the term to indicate their sexual orientation because it is largely understood by others.

Butch – (noun & adj) a person who identifies themselves as masculine, whether it be physically, mentally or emotionally. 'Butch' is sometimes used as a derogatory term for lesbians, but is also be claimed as an affirmative identity label.

Cisgender – (adj) a person whose gender identity and biological sex assigned at birth align (e.g., man and male-assigned).

- A simple way to think about it is if a person is not trans*, they are cisgender.
- "Cis" is a latin prefix that means "on the same side [as]" or "on this side [of]."

Cisnormativity – (noun) the assumption, in individuals or in institutions, that everyone is cisgender, and that cisgender identities are superior to trans* identities or people. Leads to invisibility of non-cisgender identities.

Cissexism – (noun) behavior that grants preferential treatment to cisgender people, reinforces the idea that being cisgender is somehow better or more "right" than queerness, or makes other genders invisible.

Closeted – (adj) an individual who is not open to themselves or others about their (queer) sexuality or gender identity. This may be by choice and/or for other reasons such as fear for one's safety, peer or family rejection or disapproval and/or loss of housing, job, etc. Also known as being "in the closet." When someone chooses to break this silence they "come out" of the closet. (See coming out)

Coming Out – (1) the process by which one accepts and/or comes to identify one's own sexuality or gender identity (to "come out" to oneself). (2) The process by which one shares one's sexuality or gender identity with others (to "come out" to friends, etc.).

• This is a continual, life-long process. Everyday, all the time, one has to evaluate and re-evaluate who they are comfortable coming out to, if it is safe, and what the consequences might be.

Cross-dresser – (noun) someone who wears clothes of another gender/sex.

Demi-sexual – (noun) an individual who does not experience sexual attraction unless they have formed a strong emotional connection with another individual. Often within a romantic relationship.

Drag King – (noun) someone who performs masculinity theatrically.

Drag Queen – (noun) someone who performs femininity theatrically.

Dyke – (noun) a term referring to a masculine presenting lesbian. While often used derogatorily, it can is adopted affirmatively by many lesbians (and not necessarily masculine ones) as a positive self-identity term.

Fag(got) – (noun) derogatory term referring to a gay person, or someone perceived as queer. Occasionally used as an self-identifying affirming term by some gay men, at times in the shortened form 'fag'.

Femme – (noun & adj) someone who identifies themselves as feminine, whether it be physically, mentally or emotionally. Often used to refer to a feminine-presenting lesbian.

Fluid(ity) – generally with another term attached, like gender-fluid or fluid-sexuality, fluid(ity) describes an identity that is a fluctuating mix of the options available (e.g., man and woman, bi and straight).

FTM / F2M – abbreviation for female-to-male transgender or transsexual person.

Gay – (adj) (1) a term used to describe individuals who are primarily emotionally, physically, and/or sexually attracted to members of the same sex. More commonly used when referring to males, but can be applied to females as well. (2) An umbrella term used to refer to the queer community as a whole, or as an individual identity label for anyone who does not identify as heterosexual.

- "Gay" is a word that's had many different meanings throughout time. In the 12th century is meant "happy," in the 17th century it was more commonly used to mean "immoral" (describing a loose and pleasure-seeking person), and by the 19th it meant a female prostitute (and a "gay man" was a guy who had sex with female prostitutes a lot). It wasn't until the 20th century that it started to mean what it means today. Pretty crazy.

Gender Binary – (noun) the idea that there are only two genders – male/female or man/woman and that a person must be strictly gendered as either/or.

Gender Expression – (noun) the external display of one's gender, through a combination of dress, demeanor, social behavior, and other factors, generally measured on scales of masculinity and femininity.

Gender Fluid - (adj) gender fluid is a gender identity best described as a dynamic mix of boy and girl. A person who is gender fluid may always feel like a mix of the two traditional genders, but may feel more man.

Gender Identity – (noun) the internal perception of an one's gender, and how they label themselves, based on how much they align or don't align with what they understand their options for gender to be.

- Generally confused with biological sex, or sex assigned at birth.

Gender Normative / Gender Straight – (adj) someone whose gender presentation, whether by nature or by choice, aligns with society's gender-based expectations

Genderqueer - (adj) is a catch-all term for gender identities other than man and woman, thus outside of the gender binary and cisnormativity (sometimes referred to as non-binary). People who identify as genderqueer may think of themselves as one or more of the following:

- both man and woman (bigender, pangender);
- neither man nor woman (genderless, agender);
- moving between genders (genderfluid);
- third gender or other-gendered; includes those who do not place a name to their gender;
- having an overlap of, or blurred lines between, gender identity and sexual and romantic orientation.

Gender Variant – (adj) someone who either by nature or by choice does not conform to gender-based expectations of society (e.g. transgender, transsexual, intersex, gender-queer, cross-dresser, etc.).

Gynesexual/Gynephilic – (adj) attracted to woman, females, and/or femininity.

Hermaphrodite – (noun) an outdated medical term previously used to refer someone who was born with both male and female biological characteristics; not used today as it is considered to be medically stigmatizing, and also misleading as it means a person who is 100% male and female, a biological impossibility for humans (preferred term is intersex).

Heteronormativity – (noun) the assumption, in individuals or in institutions, that everyone is heterosexual, and that heterosexuality is superior to all other sexualities. Leads to invisibility and stigmatizing of other sexualities.

Heterosexism – (noun) behavior that grants preferential treatment to heterosexual people, reinforces the idea that heterosexuality is somehow better or more "right" than queerness, or makes other sexualities invisible.

Heterosexual – (adj) a person primarily emotionally, physically, and/or sexually attracted to members of the opposite sex. Also see straight.

Homophobia – (noun) an umbrella term for a range of negative attitudes (e.g., fear, anger, intolerance, resentment, or discomfort) that one may have towards members of LGBTQ community. The term can also connote a fear, disgust, or dislike of being perceived as LGBTQ.

- The term is extended to bisexual and transgender people as well; however, the terms biphobia and transphobia are used to emphasize the specific biases against individuals of bisexual and transgender communities.

- Often experienced inwardly as an individual begins to question their own sexuality.

Homosexual – (adj) a [medical] term used to describe a person primarily emotionally, physically, and/or sexually attracted to members of the same sex. This term is considered stigmatizing due to its history as a category of mental illness, and is discouraged for common use (use gay or lesbian instead).

- Until 1973 "Homosexuality" was classified as a mental disorder in the DSM Diagnostic and Statistical Manual of Mental Disorders. This is just one of the reasons that there are such heavy negative and clinical connotations with this term.

- There was a study done prior to DADT (Don't Ask, Don't Tell) being revoked about peoples' feelings towards open queer service members. When asked, "How do you feel about open gay and lesbian service members," there was aout 65% support (at the time)." When the question was changed to, "How do you feel about open homosexual service members," the same demographic of people being asked - support drops over 20%. There are different connotations to the word homosexual then there are to gay/lesbian individuals that is powerful and salient both to straight and queer people.

Intersex – (adj) someone whose combination of chromosomes, gonads, hormones, internal sex organs, and genitals differs from the two expected patterns of male or female. Formerly known as hermaphrodite (or hermaphroditic), but these terms are now considered outdated and derogatory.

- Often seen as a problematic condition when babies or young children are identified as intersex, it was for a long term considered an "emergency" and something that doctors moved to "fix" right away in a newborn child. There has been increasing advocacy and awareness brought to this issue and many individuals advocate that intersex individuals should be allowed to remain intersex past infancy and to not treat the condition as an issue or medical emergency.

Lesbian – (noun) a term used to describe women attracted romantically, erotically, and/or emotionally to other women.

- The term lesbian is derived from the name of the Greek island of Lesbos and as such is sometimes considered a Eurocentric category that does not necessarily represent the identities of Black women and other non-European ethnic groups.
- Many individual women from diverse ethnic groups, including Black women, embrace the term "lesbian" as an identity label.
- While many women use the term lesbian, many women also will describe themselves as gay, this is a personal choice. Many prefer the term gay because of its use in adjective form.

Lipstick Lesbian – (noun) Usually refers to a lesbian with a feminine gender expression. Can be used in a positive or a derogatory way. Is sometimes also used to refer to a lesbian who is assumed to be (or passes for) straight.

Metrosexual – (noun & adj) a straight man with a strong aesthetic sense who spends more time, energy, or money on his appearance and grooming than is considered gender normative.

MTF/ M2F – abbreviation from male-to-female transgender or transsexual person.

Outing – (verb) involuntary or unwanted disclosure of another person's sexual orientation, gender identity, or intersex status.

Pansexual – (adj) a person who experiences sexual, romantic, physical, and/or spiritual attraction for members of all gender identities/expressions.

Passing – (verb) (1) a term for trans* people being accepted as, or able to "pass for," a member of their self- identified gender/sex identity (regardless of birth sex). (2) An LGB/queer individual who can is believed to be or perceived as straight.

- While for many trans* people this considered to be a positive experience and allows them to reveal their trans* identity only at their own discretion, for many queer individuals passing is not a positive experience as it may feel invalidating or make them feel invisible within their own community.

Polyamory – (noun) refers to having honest, usual non-possessive, relationships with multiple partners and can include: open relationships, polyfidelity (which involves multiple romantic relationships with sexual contact restricted to those), and sub-relationships (which denote distinguishing between a 'primary' relationship or relationships and various "secondary" relationships).

Preferred Gender Pronouns (PGPs) – (noun) a phrase used as an affirmative way of asking someone how they would like to be referred to (common examples: she/her/hers, he/him/his, they/them/theirs, ze/zir/zirs).

Queer – (adj) used as an umbrella term to describe individuals who identify as non-straight. Also used to describe people who have non-normative gender identity or as a political affiliation. Due to its historical use as a derogatory term, it is not embraced or used by all members of the LGBTQ community. The term queer can often be use interchangeably with LGBTQ.

- If a person tells you they are not comfortable with you referring to them as queer, don't. Always respect individual's preferences when it comes to identity labels, particularly contentious ones (or ones with troubled histories) like this.

- Use the word queer only if you are comfortable explaining to others what it means, because some people feel uncomfortable with the word, it is best to know/feel comfortable explaining why you choose to use it if someone inquires.

Questioning – (verb, adjective) an individual who is unsure about or is exploring their own sexual orientation or gender identity.

Same Gender Loving / SGL – (adj) a term sometimes used by members of the African-American / Black community to express an alternative sexual orientation without relying on terms and symbols of European descent.

Sex Assigned At Birth – (noun) a phrase used to intentionally recognize a person's assigned sex, often abbreviated SAAB (or FAAB, "female assigned at birth"; and MAAB, "male assigned at birth).

Sexual Orientation – (noun) the type of sexual, romantic, physical, and/or spiritual attraction one feels for others, often labeled based on the gender relationship between the person and the people they are attracted to (often mistakenly referred to as sexual preference).

Sexual Preference – (1) the types of sexual intercourse, stimulation, and gratification one likes to receive and participate in. (2) Generally when this term is used, it is being mistakenly interchanged with "sexual orientation," creating an illusion that one has a choice (or "preference") in who they are attracted to.

Sex Reassignment Surgery / SRS – A term used by some medical professionals to refer to a group of surgical options that alter a person's biological sex. In most cases, one or multiple surgeries are required to achieve legal recognition of gender variance. "Gender confirmation surgery" is considered to me a more affirmative term.

Skoliosexual – (adj) attracted to genderqueer and transsexual people and expressions (people who don't identify as cisgender).

Straight – (adj) a person primarily emotionally, physically, and/or sexually attracted to members of the opposite sex. A more colloquial term for the word heterosexual.

Stud – (noun) an African-American and/of Latina masculine lesbian. Also known as 'butch' or 'aggressive'. Top Surgery – (noun) this term refers to surgery for the construction of a male-type chest or breast augmentation for a female-type chest.

Trans* – (noun) an umbrella term for people whose gender identity and/or gender expression differs from the sex they were assigned at birth. Trans* people may identify with a particular descriptive term (e.g., transgender, transsexual, genderqueer, FTM).

Transgender – (1) An umbrella term covering a range of identities that transgress socially defined gender norms; (2) (adj) A person who lives as a member of a gender other than that expected based on anatomical sex.

- Because sexuality labels (e.g., gay, straight, bi) are generally based on the relationship between the person's gender and the genders they are attracted to, trans* sexuality can be defined in a couple of ways. Some people may choose to self-identify as straight, gay, bi, lesbian, or pansexual (or others, using their gender identity as a basis), or they might describe their sexuality using other-focused terms like gynesexual, androsexual, or skoliosexual.

Transition(ing) – (noun & verb) this term is primarily used to refer to the process a trans* person undergoes when changing their bodily appearance either to be more congruent with the gender/sex they feel themselves to be and/or to be in harmony with their preferred gender expression.

Transman – (noun) An identity label sometimes adopted by female-to-male transgender people or transsexuals to signify that they are men while still affirming their history as females. (sometimes referred to as transguy)

Transphobia –(noun) the fear of, discrimination against, or hatred of trans* people, the trans* community, or gender ambiguity. Transphobia can be seen within the queer community, as well as in general society.

Transsexual – (noun & adj) a person who identifies psychologically as a gender/sex other than the one to which they were assigned at birth. Transsexuals often wish to transform their bodies hormonally and surgically to match their inner sense of gender/sex.

Transvestite – (noun) a person who dresses as the binary opposite gender expression ("cross-dresses") for any one of many reasons, including relaxation, fun, and sexual gratification (often called a "cross-dresser," and should not be confused with transsexual).

Transwoman – (noun) an identity label sometimes adopted by male-to-female transsexuals or transgender people to signify that they are women while still affirming their history as males.

Two-Spirit – (noun) is a term traditionally used by Native American people to recognize individuals who possess qualities or fulfill roles of both women and men.

- Being "two-spirit" was traditionally considered an honor, and a mark of wisdom, instead of being viewed as a stigma that it is in other cultures.

Ze / Hir – alternate pronouns that are gender neutral and preferred by some trans* people.

- Pronounced /zee/ and /here/ they replace "he" and "she" and "his" and "hers" respectively.
- Alternatively some people who are not comfortable/do not embrace he/she use the plural pronoun "they/their" as a gender neutral singular pronoun.

TRANS*

WHAT DOES THE * STAND FOR?

*TRANSGENDER
*TRANSSEXUAL *TRANSVESTITE
*GENDERQUEER
*GENDERFLUID *NON-BINARY *GENDERF*CK
*GENDERLESS
*AGENDER *NON-GENDERED
*THIRD GENDER
*TWO-SPIRIT * BIGENDER
*TRANS MAN
*TRANS WOMAN

APPENDIX B

TRANS* ASTERISK

IF YOU CAN'T BE KIND, AT LEAST BE VAGUE.

—Judith Manners

You've likely noticed my frequent use of "trans*" throughout the book, instead of "trans" or "transgender." What is this? Why do I do it? What does it all mean?

Allow me to explain.

AN UMBRELLA OF UMBRELLAS

Trans* is an umbrella term that refers to all of the non-binary identities within the gender identity spectrum. There's a ton of diversity there, but we often group them all together (e.g., when we say "trans* issues).

Trans (without the asterisk) is often considered to be an umbrella term as well, but it's also often used as a general term for trans men and trans women. Transgender, similarly, is considered by many to be an umbrella term, but there are individuals who identify solely as "transgender," so that could lead to some confusion when using "transgender" to refer to all non-binary gender identities.

The asterisk makes special note in an effort to include all non-binary gender identities, including transgender, transsexual, transvestite, genderqueer, genderfluid, non-binary, neutrois, genderfuck, genderless, agender, non-gendered, third gender, two-spirit, bigender, and trans man and trans woman.

WHY AN ASTERISK?

The origin behind the asterisk, as I understand it, is a bit computer geeky. When you add an asterisk to the end of a search term, you're telling your computer to search for whatever you typed, plus any characters after (e.g., [search term*][extra letters], or trans*[-gender, -queer, -sexual, etc.]). The idea was to include trans and other identities related to trans, in the most technically awesome way. I heart geekdom.

The asterisk is also a great way to denote this specific usage becasue in writing asterisks usually signify some fine print or exception to what you're saying. For example, if you were to say free*, people would immediately know you don't mean whatever you're talking about is necessarily free, and that some conditions may need to be satisfied. Trans* catches the eye in a similar way, and gives the reader pause to consider the implications of the asterisk.

The pause evoked by the asterisk is a great way to evoke the mindfulness of the comprehensive nature with which you are using that term. While "transgender" or "trans" might accomplish inclusivity for some, others may think you are talking about those individual identities respectively, carrying in their own predispositions as they read whatever you're writing.

TO * OR NOT TO *

There is a debate on the interwebs about whether the asterisk is helping or hurting, necessary or superfluous, helpful or redundant, Team Jacob or Team Edward. I'm on the side that says it's helpful (obviously), and Team Edward (obviously), but I also want to give you a glimpse of some of the arguments against it to best prepare you to make your own decision to asterisk or not to asterisk.

One of the main arguments against the asterisk (and the one I find to be the weightiest) is that it leads to further segmentation of the community, which hinders progress and unity. Adding the asterisk creates a separate term, which means something different from transgender or trans, and, in turn, creates another group of people that folks not familiar with transgender people or issues need to learn about.

But there are other arguments as well. One is that it's unnecessary to use the asterisk, stating that "trans" was already meant to be an all-encompassing term. Or that the asterisk leads to confusion in print because it generally signifies a footnote. Some people are more fond of a hyphen ("trans-") because they think it better demonstrates the idea of it being one beginning for many endings. And there are some folks who just plain think it's ugly.

While I encourage the use of the asterisk, the choice to use or not use it (as with all of my recomendations) is entirely yours*.

*Prices and participation may vary.

APPENDIX C

RECOMMENDED READING

ALWAYS READ SOMETHING THAT WILL MAKE YOU LOOK GOOD IF YOU
DIE IN THE MIDDLE OF IT.

—*P.J. O'Rourke*

Throughout the book, I mentioned a lot of other folks' work I've enjoyed, research I've found to be helpful, and other works that were worth mentioning. Beyond that, there is a lot of work that I don't explicitly reference but has shaped my lens and helped me form my perspective on all of this gender stuff. This appendix is a collection of many of those thing for your future learning and lens shaping, and I will keep a running reading list going on the website www.guideto-gender.com if you're looking for more.

BOOKS & ARTICLES

1,138 Benefits of Marriage. Human Rights Campaign. http://www.hrc.org/resources/entry/an-overview-of-federal-rights-and-protections-granted-to-married-couples

Angier, Natalie. Woman: an intimate geography. Boston: Houghton Mifflin Co., 1999.

Bernburg, Jön G. and Krohn, Marvin D. Labeling, life chances, and adult crime: The direct and indirect effects of official intervention in adolescence on crime in early adulthood. Criminology, 2003.

Brafman, Ori, and Rom Brafman. Sway: the irresistible pull of irrational behavior. New York: Doubleday, 2008.

Butler, Judith. Gender trouble: feminism and the subversion of identity. New York: Routledge, 1990.

Butler, Judith. Undoing gender. New York: Routledge, 2004.

Cheryan, Sapna, and Bodenhausen, Galen V. When positive stereotypes threaten intellectual performance: The psychological hazards of "model minority" status. American Psychological Society, 2000.

Ehrensaft, Diane. Gender born, gender made: raising healthy gender-nonconforming children. New York: Experiment, 2011.

Eugenides, Jeffrey. Middlesex. New York: Farrar, Straus, Giroux, 2002.

Fine, Cordelia. Delusions of gender: how our minds, society, and neurosexism create difference. New York: W. W. Norton, 2010.

Halberstam, Judith. In a queer time and place: transgender bodies, subcultural lives. New York: New York University Press, 2005.

Kinsey, Alfred C., Wardell Baxter Pomeroy, and Clyde E. Martin. Sexual behavior in the human male. Philadelphia: W.B. Saunders Co., 1948.

McIntosh, Peggy. White privilege and male privilege: a personal account of coming to see correspondences through work in women's studies. Wellesley, MA: Wellesley College, Center for Research on Women, 1988.

Reason, Robert D.. Developing social justice allies. San Francisco: Jossey-Bass, 2005.

Serano, Julia. Whipping girl: a transsexual woman on sexism and the scapegoating of femininity. Emeryville, CA: Seal Press, 2007.

Simpson, Mark. Male impersonators: men performing masculinity. New York, NY: Routledge, 1994.

Steinem, Gloria. Outrageous acts and everyday rebellions. New York: Holt, Rinehart, and Winston, 1983.

Sterling, Anne. Sexing the body: gender politics and the construction of sexuality. New York, NY: Basic Books, 2000.

Tannen, Deborah. Gender and conversational interaction. New York: Oxford University Press, 1993.

Tannen, Deborah. Gender and discourse. New York: Oxford University Press, 1994.

INTERWEBZ

Everyday Feminism. Daily articles that help readers apply intersectional feminism in their lives. http://everydayfeminism.com

It's Pronounced Metrosexual. Articles and graphics about gender, sexuality, and social justice. http://itspronouncedmetrosexual.com

The Safe Zone Project. An online resource for creating powerful, effective LGBTQ education an ally training workshops. http://thesafezoneproject.com

Transwhat? A collection of how-tos and educational pieces for would-be trans* allies. http://transwhat.org/

WikiQueer. Like Wikipedia, but just for queer stuff! http://www.wikiqueer.org/

HEARTFELT THANKS

THROWN OVER A PRECIPICE, YOU FALL OR ELSE YOU FLY.

—*Margaret Atwood*

My days usually start early. I wake up to my phone, in my bed, rolling around to avoid the morning light creeping through my blinds as I read E-mails & Twitters & Facebooks that have accumulated over the previous few hours while I dreamt. Then I hop on my bicycle, ride to a coffee shop, and get to work on whatever work I have in store for that day—generally some little project that I hope will make the world a better place.

Some argue that I never wake up—that I am living my dream. But this job I have, if we're going to call it that, was never my dream. I wouldn't have dared dream so boldly. I didn't even know this was a *thing*, let alone a thing I could *be*. But the slipper fit, and now here I am, being swept off my feet every morning as I wake up to a life I owe—in more ways than I can say—to all you Prince Charmings.

It's through my writing that I've been able to learn much of what I know. It is through the discussions that happen online, via e-mail, or in comments sections of the articles I write, that all of the grayness of identity becomes a little more black and white, or, rather, a higher fidelity of gray.

I believe in what I do. There is harmony in my life, as my head, my heart, and my work all sing different parts of the same song—a song that keeps me smiling every day, even if some days it's more melancholy than cheerful. And yes, I absolutely do believe that it's possible for us to create a world that is socially just. It's already happening. We're making it happen.

There are some specific people to whom I owe specific thank yous, but I also want to broadly thank everyone who has ever linked to one of my articles, shared one of my little doodles with a friend, or seen my show at a college. Thank you for helping me fly.

Never ask for permission to smile,

sK

Thank you to my patient, critical, and (in many cases) hilarious pool of content editors (guinea pigs) for allowing me to test this book on you, and for putting up with me and my silliness through countless rounds of revisions and countless volumes of silliness:

KATE DONNELLY - COREY BERNSTEIN - CHRISTINE ADAME - LEIGH NIEMAN - ERIC MORROW - GABI CLAYTON - REUBS WALSH - CC ALEXANDER - JJ JIMENEZ - PAUL REINERFELT - KATH COOPER - CARL HOLLAMBY - KATRINA LEWIS - KIERAN HIXON - MARY VANCE - NATASHA COX - ABBY ROSENSTEIN - MICHELLE SIMS - STEPHANIE JONES - DEVON GUIDOUX - JENN GALLIENNE, CANDACE JACKSON - VICKY HUMMEL - SARAH VILLARROEL - LISA HAMBLEN - ZEE HILDRETH - ELISA KANO - FRAN FUDGE - KARINA OGUNLANA

Thank you to the coffee shops that provided me a home away from home in Austin, giving me the space and comfort I needed to write, edit, & design this book.

And special thanks to the smiling staff who were there to give me the push (caffeine, usually) I needed to keep moving (jittering, usually):

BOULDIN CREEK CAFE

&

THE HIDEOUT THEATRE COFFEE HOUSE

&

TOM'S TABOOLEY

Thank you to my patient, supportive, and encouraging financiers of the publishing of this book who took a leap over a precipice themselves, putting their faith in me and this project:

AARON C SLUSHER - AARON CHRISTINE FULMEK - AIDAN FORTIER - AL VERNACCHIO - ALBERT RICHARD MAYA - ALBINA VELTMAN - ALEX BURSLEM - ALEXANDRA BROWN - ALICE NUTTALL - ALICE TUCKEY - AMELIA NAUGLER - AMIE MCKIBBAN - AMY DONAHUE - AMY ELMGREN - AMY MILLIGAN - AMY SHEARER - ANA VARGAS-MACHUCA - ANDERSON TEMPLETON - ANDREW BECKNELL - ANDREW HUGHES - ANDY SEMLER - ANGIE BADE - ANNEMARIE SHROUDER - ANNETTE MARQUIS - APRIL NANCE - ASHLEE FERRET - BARBARA FINDLAY - BETH MITCHELL - BETH SHAW - BETH WILSON - BEVIN TIGHE - BRIAN JARA - BUGS - LESIA QUAMINA - NIKITA MITCHELL - CAILIN HAYES - CALLUM - CANDACE ALEXANDRA PRICE - CARL HOLLAMBY - CARLY LYES - CATIA AGUIAR - CHAMINDA MAPA - CHANDRA ALTOFF - CHARLIE MURRAY - CHRIS ALEXANDER - CODY RICHARD - COURTNEY M WATSON - COURTNEY THAMAN - CRAIG LEETS - DAN MOSORA - DANIEL SILVERSTONE - DANNA COOKE - DARA HOFFMAN-FOX - DAVID CAMERON - DEL RAPIER - DENISE CROSS - DENISE HUESO - DENISE MURRAY - DORAN STUCKY - DR. TREVOR CORNEIL - EDWARD BARTOW - ELANA GELLER - ELISSA DIAZ - ELIZABETH TRAN - ELLEN CREGAN - ELOISE STONBOROUGH - EMI SHAW COLORADO - EMILY SWAIN - ENNE ILO PUROVAARA - ERICA JONES - ERICA M. JONES - ERIKA BRIDGEFORTH - ERIN SUBRAMANIAN - ERIN-CLAIRE BARROW - GAIL DUNN - GERY MURCHAKE - GIA CAMPANELLA SCHNEIDER - GILLIAN - GILLIAN CALDER - GINA PATTERSON - GUINEVERE JEANETTE OCTOBER - HANNAH HOWARTH - HEATHER SANKEY - HEATHER WEHR - HELEN BISHOP - HELMUTH BREITENFELLNER - HOLLY ELIJAH - IAN TENNANT - JACKIE MCCLANAHAN - JAKE KOPMEIER - JAMES BUCKLEY - JAROD WILSON - JASREET BADYAL - JEFF SMITH - JEFFREY CHUSB - JEN SALAMONE - JESSE FUCHS - JESSICA D EARLEY - JESSICA GRIFFITH - JESSICA LANGLOIS - JESSICA WOODS - JO FOY - JOAN GARRITY - JODI SHIPLEY - JOHN WARREN - JONATHAN HARDY - JORDAN STRYK - JOY BUTLER - JULIA BERBERAN - JUSTIN KALINAU - KAITY WERNER - KARA SJOBLOM-BAY - KAREN GOLD - KAREN IZZI GALLAGHER - KAREN THORSON - KAROLYN CHOWNING - KATE HAUSER - KATHLEEN HARRISON - KATHRYN SWEENEY - KATRINA LEWIS - KERRI HURMAN - KEVIN MOHABIR - KIER SINCLAIR - KRISTA ROYAL - KRISTEN GILBERT - KRISTEN STUBBS - KRISTINA VANHEESWIJK - KRISTINE ERICKSON - KRYSTINA COLTON - LAURA DELLOSTRITTO - LENNY GREY - LENORA PEYTON - LIAT NORRIS - LINDA EISENSTEIN - LIS MAURER - LISA RUIGROK - LISA SALAZAR - LISA SCHULZE - LN YOUNG - LUCIAN CLARK - LUKYAN BEX ALLES - M. SORGE - MALIA LEWIS - MANSI KATHURIA - MARIA E DOERFLER - MARIE DIPPENAAR - MARION CROMB - MARTHA FISCHHOFF - MARY NEATON - MARY VANCE - MAYA PILGRIM - MEGAN GOODWIN - MEGAN MCRAE - MIAH AKSTON - MICA GONZALEZ - MICHAEL LEICESTER - MICHAEL SKAANING - MICHAELA KIRBY - MICHELE REN - MICHELLE RATNAYEKE - MIKE MOSS - MORGAN PURRIER - MORGEN CHANG - NANCY WOODS - NATALIE MILLMAN - NICO KERSKI - OLIVER MCKEON - ORR GULAT - PAULA KAMPF - PRECIOUS PORRAS - RACHEL CRANE - RACHEL ELLIS - REBECCA LEYS - REBECCA WHITTIER - REMY LOURENCO - RENE WINEGAR - RIOT MUELLER - ROBIN WILSON - RUFAI AJALA - SAL PEARSON - SALLY CONNING - SAMANTHA MARGERISON - SANDRA RICHARD - SARAH JEAN TAAVOLA - SARAH SMITH - SARAH SMITH - SEAMUS JOHNSTON - SEAN BARRETT - SEAN EDDINGTON - SEFIK A MAI - SEVAN MARLOW BUSSELL - SHAUNA WOODARD - SHELBY LAVIGNA - STEPHANIE RICKETTS - STEPHANIE SMITH - TANJA JACOBS - TEGAN STOVER - TERRI COOK - TERYL BERG - THALIDA NOEL - THEODORE DRAKE WARD - TONY DEAN - TRAVIS AMIEL - TUNAN PAN - VANYA LARSEN LUNDIN - ZARA STEADMAN - ZOYA STREET

ABOUT THE AUTHOR

Sam Killermann is a comedian and social justice advocate, and the guy behind *It's Pronounced Metrosexual*, a one-man comedy show and blog about snap judgments, identity, and oppression (but in a totally funny way). He travels the country performing the show at colleges and universities, and writes articles about social justice, gender, and sexuality when he's not on the road. His work has appeared in the *New York Times*, *The Atlantic*, and your Facebook news feed.

Sam's obsession with understanding gender comes from his own experiences with gender and sexuality. He's constantly incorrectly assumed to be gay, which has everything to do with his gender and little-to-nothing to do with his sexuality. Gender is one of those things everyone thinks they understand, but most don't really understand at all. Kind of like the usage of the word "irony" (isn't that ironic?).

As a self-labeled "social justice comedian," he spends a lot of his time trying to prove to people that this label makes sense. Sam is a dedicated ally and advocate, and blends humor into much of the work he does because he believes (like Mary Poppins believed) that sugar helps the medicine go down.

Outside of *It's Pronounced Metrosexual*, Sam runs a non-profit he founded called *Gamers Against Bigotry*, is the co-creator of *The Safe Zone Project*, is always working on new social good projects, and likes to spend a least a couple hours a day cycling around sunny Austin, TX, where he counts himself as lucky to live.